Varig
Star of Brazil

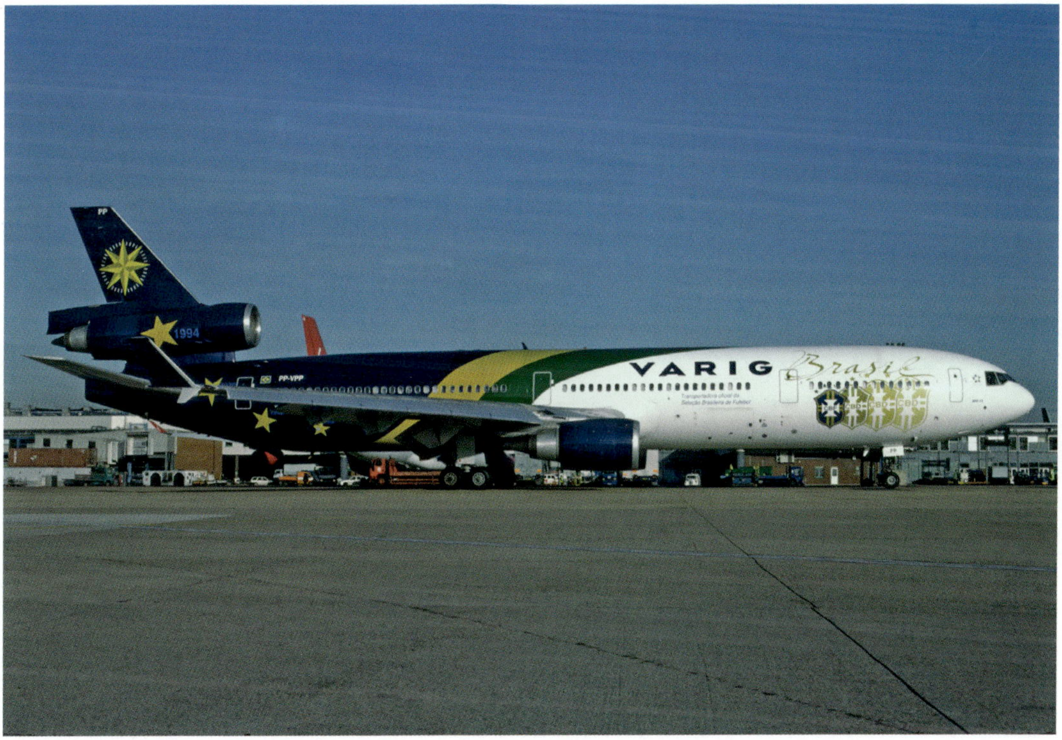

BARRY LLOYD

KEY
Books

AIRLINES SERIES, VOLUME 6

Front cover image: MD 11 PP VTK on final approach to Heathrow. The aircraft was converted to a freighter in 2007, after the demise of Varig. (Richard Vandervord)

Contents page image: A typical 1980s scene at São Paulo's Congonhas airport, showing its close proximity to the city centre. (Bob O'Brien Collection)

Published by Key Books
An imprint of Key Publishing Ltd
PO Box 100
Stamford
Lincs PE19 1XQ

www.keypublishing.com

The rights of Barry Lloyd to be identified as the author of this book has been asserted in accordance with the Copyright, Designs and Patents Act 1988 Sections 77 and 78.

Copyright © Barry Lloyd, 2022

ISBN 978 1 80282 250 2

All rights reserved. Reproduction in whole or in part in any form whatsoever or by any means is strictly prohibited without the prior permission of the Publisher.

Typeset by SJmagic DESIGN SERVICES, India.

Contents

Introduction

When the Portuguese landed in Brazil on 22 April 1500, they could not have imagined what riches they would ultimately discover. In the northeast of the country, a Portuguese fleet, commanded by Pedro Alves Cabral, encountered small tribes of people who spoke their own Indigenous languages and fought regularly among themselves. The first Portuguese settlement was founded in 1532, but colonisation of the country did not begin until 1534, when King John III of Portugal divided up the territory. However, this proved problematic, and the King then restructured them into the Governorate General of Brazil, making Salvador the country's capital. The capital later moved to Rio de Janeiro and, in 1960, to Brasilia, the city conceived by former president, Juscelino Kubitschek.

The name Brazil is attributed to the brazilwood tree, which grows along the Atlantic coast. The wood it produces is red, and the word 'Brazil' comes from the Portuguese word for embers. Brazil was originally called Terra da Santa Cruz (Land of the Holy Cross).

Initially, Brazil was settled mainly in the coastal areas. This involved working the sugar plantations to satisfy the huge European demand for sugar, the harvesting of which is very labour intensive and thus required a large amount of imported labour, which was brought from Africa. Brazil shipped in more than 500,000 enslaved people to work in the sugar cane fields and also in the mines. Shipments of gold from Brazil were so substantial that the country was able to supply half of the global demand, which brought almost 400,000 migrants from Portugal to Brazil in the 18th century. In addition to the Portuguese, there was substantial migration of people from many different countries, including many from Europe. This has played a huge part in shaping the cultural and social aspects of present-day Brazil, which must rank as one of the world's most ethnically diverse countries.

In addition to gold, the mines contained bauxite, precious stones of many different varieties, platinum and other rare minerals. A significant gold rush began in earnest the 1960s, following its discovery in the area of Belo Horizonte. This had been preceded by a diamond rush in 1729, after precious stones were discovered in the same region, known as Minas Gerais (general mines). Today, Brazil still has a huge mining sector. Principal amongst these is iron-ore, bauxite (for aluminium), manganese and tin, amongst others. In addition, precious minerals such as amethyst, topaz, emerald and opal are found in specific areas.

Brazil is the world's largest producer of many agricultural products, including sugar cane, coffee, and oranges, and is one of the top five producers of cotton, pineapples, beans, coconuts and maize. It also produces significant quantities of avocados, mangoes, rice, and tomatoes. Additional products supplied by the agricultural sector also include grapes, apples, melons, onions and palm oil. It is a measure of how diverse Brazil's climate is that such a wide variety of produce is grown. The mega figures do not just relate to agriculture. In 2019, it was the world's largest exporter of chicken meat, the second largest producer of beef and seventh largest producer of eggs.

Brazil is famous as the world's largest producer of coffee, but it is perhaps surprising to learn that it is among the top ten oil producers, supplying more than Iran or Kuwait. Until 1997, the government had a monopoly in the sector, but more than 50 companies participate in the industry today. The largest oil producing company is the multinational Petrobras, which alone produces at least 2 million barrels of oil daily. In 2006, the country's oil reserves were second only to Venezuela among South American countries. Most of the reserves are located in places like Santos and Campos in São Paulo state. Although Brazil exports oil, it also imports oil, not least because demand outstrips supply, but the need for importation also arises from the fact that the country's infrastructure for oil refining is outdated. Many of the refineries were built in the 1960s and are now incapable of handling the heavy nature of the oil currently found in Brazil. The heavy oil that is found there today had not been discovered when the plants were being built.

The international mass migration from Europe to Brazil during the 19th century was also instrumental in the country's development. The influx of immigrants brought a mix of cultures, experiences, and knowledge to their new country. The regions where the most immigrants settled saw a jump in growth and productivity.

Whilst the remainder of the Spanish-speaking Americas fragmented into many different republics following their independence from Spain, Brazil remained a single administrative unit, thus making it the largest country in Latin America. It is not widely realised, but in terms of area, Brazil is only slightly smaller than the US – 8,100,200 square miles (3,127,500 square km) compared to 9,833,520 square miles (3,796,742 square km). For example, a direct flight between Porto Alegre, the largest city in the south, to Boa Vista, the largest city in the north, typically takes more than four and a half hours. The spread of the country is such that it spans an area from north of the Equator to well below the Tropic of Capricorn. Because of this, it can be understood that the country has many differing climates, but despite its natural mineral wealth and ability to produce huge quantities and varieties of food, Brazil has regularly suffered throughout its history from economic and political problems, often resulting in rampant inflation. As recently as 1990, the rate of inflation reached a staggering 2,590 per cent. The currency constantly devalues against the US dollar, and, since 1942, Brazil has changed the name and status of its currency eight times, invariably as the result of inflation.

The early Republican government was little more than a military dictatorship, with the country effectively being run by the army. Civilian governments were in power between 1894 and 1930. In late 1930, President Getúlio Vargas, who had risen to power with the backing of the military, had the intention of breaking the political dominance of the coffee producers. With an election due in 1938, Vargas could not technically seek re-election, but he was unwilling to pass the reins of power to anyone else. Vargas went to the military, and with its backing, was able to re-take power. Vargas ruled as a dictator, but, eventually, even the military tired of his authoritarian rule, which was ended in October 1945, after 15 years in power. President Eurico Dutra replaced him and held power from 1946 to 1951 and was re-elected democratically between 1951 and 1954. Vargas committed suicide on 24 August 1954. There followed a short-term series of largely ineffective presidents between 1954 and 1964, including Juscelino Kubitschek, which was enough to persuade the military to take power again. On 1 April 1964, following a coup d'état by the Brazilian Armed Forces, the military took power of all aspects of Brazilian life. The military government remained in power for more than 20 years, until 15 March 1985.

It was against this unstable political and economic background that Varig found itself operating on a day-to-day basis. The ever-changing political situation meant that the Brazilian currency suffered constant minor devaluations. This is difficult enough to manage in a domestic situation, but given that in the world of international aviation many of the costs – aircraft, spare parts, fuel when bought overseas, and often training on new aircraft – must be paid in US dollars, the problem is compounded to a much greater degree. Naturally, much of Varig's income was derived within Brazil, and for the most part, the airline was able to juggle its finances to enable it to pay its bills, both domestic and foreign. However, as will be seen later, this ultimately became a significant factor in the downfall of the airline. Whilst Varig normally had tacit support, both politically and economically, from the government, it was never fully nationalised in the way that other South American carriers were when they found themselves in financial difficulties.

Despite the difficulties of operating in such an unstable financial climate, there was never any shortage of potential airline operators, and therefore competition, within Brazil, some of which came and went while others that lasted for decades. The rail transport system is similar to that of the US, where there has never been a widespread passenger-carrying railway network. Road journeys within Brazil can be slow, sometimes on unpaved roads and subject to extreme weather conditions, so in many cases, flying is the most practical option. As an example, the distance by air between Rio de Janeiro and Manaus is typically 1,771 miles (2,850km), while the driving distance would be 2,685 miles (4,305km). The flight typically takes about four hours, whereas a car journey could take up to two and a half days. Additionally, there are believed to be about 2,500 airfields in Brazil, making it second only to the US in terms of numbers.

Despite the political and economic fluctuations, an entrepreneurial spirit exists in Brazil, which is largely unmatched elsewhere in South America and despite the economic and political setbacks, the country continues to drive forward at a relentless pace. The word *Bandeirante* is frequently heard in Brazil. Derived from the Portuguese word for flag, *bandeira,* it is often used to mean explorer or pioneer. The Bandeirante was the first aircraft produced by Brazilian aerospace manufacturer Embraer in 1968, and it is worth noting that Embraer has now grown to become the world's third largest producer of commercial aircraft, behind Boeing and Airbus. It is just one example of the product of an enterprising spirit. During the late 20th century and leading into the 21st century, Brazil has become an industrial and commercial powerhouse and continues to develop. For this, considerable credit must be given to the Brazilian airlines, and Varig in particular, which were instrumental in opening up a large and diverse country, often in the most difficult of circumstances, and whose commerce had originally clung to a narrow, but extensive, piece of Atlantic coastline.

As will become apparent in the concluding chapter, Varig, having survived matters beyond its control, such as the constant political upheavals and rampant inflation, was finally undone by relentless competition and its unwillingness to adapt to the newer practices taking place in aviation. Thus, the premier airline of Latin America, and one of the oldest, was forced into liquidation in 2006, after almost 80 years of operation.

Chapter 1

Small Beginnings, 1927–45

O tto Ernst Meyer had been a pilot on the Eastern Front during World War One. At that time, the Eastern Front stretched from the Baltic Sea in the north to deep into Central Europe. In 1921, at the age of 24, Meyer emigrated to Brazil to work for a textile company, initially choosing Recife in the northeastern state of Pernambuco as his home. He quickly saw the need for aircraft to traverse the vast country and approached the state governments of both Pernambuco and Rio de Janeiro for support, but he found no enthusiasm for his ideas.

After moving to Porto Alegre in Rio Grande do Sul, the most southerly state in Brazil, Meyer soon recognised the need for better transport to replace the horse-drawn vehicles that were used to transport passengers and mail between the three towns of Porto Alegre, Pelotas and Rio Grande, which surrounded a large lagoon, known locally as Lagoa dos Patos – Lake of the Ducks. In September 1926, Meyer returned to Germany and, through his contacts, was able to arrange for the Lufthansa subsidiary, Condor Syndikat, to contribute a Dornier Do J Wal (Whale) flying boat to his enterprise in exchange for 20 per cent of the shares in the newly formed company. The Wal was a twin-engined high-winged flying boat, with the engines mounted in tandem and fitted with tractor and pusher propellers, one on either end. It was capable of carrying about ten people or a cargo of about one tonne. It arrived in Rio Grande do Sul on 19 November 1926, having been shipped from Hamburg to Montevideo, where it was subsequently assembled and flown to Buenos Aires. On 27 November 1926, the aircraft, named *Atlántico* and still wearing its German registration, D-1012, arrived in Guanabara Bay in Rio de Janeiro, flown by a German crew, as part of a demonstration tour.

In early January 1927, the aircraft took part in one of a series of flights from Rio to Florianópolis via Santos. On 29 January, *Atlántico* left for Porto Alegre on a positioning flight. On board was Meyer. The next big event was on 3 February, when the aircraft, having been christened whilst operating in the Spanish-speaking countries, had its name amended slightly to *Atlântico*, in order to reflect the difference between Spanish and Portuguese, before making the first commercial flight in Brazil on what became known as the 'Lagoon Line'. The initial flights were made under the title of Condor Syndikat with a German crew, and the aircraft continued to carry its German registration.

The scheduled services did not begin until 22 February 1927, enabling *Atlântico* to be refurbished. On 15 June 1927, both the aircraft and the route, from Porto Alegre to Rio Grande do Sul and Pelotas, were formally transferred from Condor Syndikat to the newly formed airline, with the first flight under its new owners taking place on 22 June. The company had been founded on May 7 1927 and named Sociedade Anônima Empresa de Viação Aérea Rio-Grandense – Varig. The name was formed from the Brazilian Portuguese words **V**iação **A**érea **Riog**randense, which translates essentially to Rio Grande Airways. Using 'Vario' would not have worked, since this means 'various' in Brazilian Portuguese.

With the name Varig now officially registered under the laws of Rio Grande do Sul, and with capitalisation provided by private investors and Condor Syndikat, the airline was now a formal entity. A little more than a month later, Varig formally received its certificate of incorporation. On 15 June,

The Dornier Wal, as it was originally operated by Varig. (Varig.com)

Atlântico was placed onto the Brazilian civil aircraft register as P-BAAA and entered as number one in the Brazilian Aeronautical Register, with the operator shown as Varig.

On 22 June 1927, the first official Varig flight was operated, connecting Porto Alegre, Pelotas and Rio Grande. *Atlântico* was taken out of service for repairs to the wing skin on 13 July of that year and replaced by a Junkers G 24, P-BABA, which was leased from Condor from 24 September. It continued to fly with Varig until 2 July 1930, when it was transferred back to Condor Syndikat. Varig's first logo was a stylised Cormorant, a seabird regularly found along the southern coast of Brazil, but this was replaced by the image of Icarus in 1930.

In these times, air travel was a unique experience, and the general public were wary of it. The task facing Varig was to convince people of the wider benefits of air travel, apart from the obvious advantage of speed. Nevertheless, air travel was still very primitive. For example, in order to board the aircraft, the passengers were taken to the docks, from where they would be transported by boat to Ilha Grande dos Marinheiros near Rio Grande where their tickets would be checked. On the ticket would be a written warning: 'For your safety, smoking is strictly prohibited, as well as throwing objects out of the windows.' The passengers would then be weighed, and anyone who weighed more the 75kg would have to pay a surcharge. The crew would wear heavy coats, together with leather helmets and goggles, since they flew in an open cockpit. The passengers flew in greater comfort in a closed cabin with comfortable seats, cotton wool available to reduce the noise, and chewing gum to help alleviate the effects of pressure changes. The boat that was used to take the passengers out would then, quite literally, make waves, to assist with the take-off.

Varig received its second aircraft in October 1927, a Dornier Merkur (Mercury). This was also a seaplane (originally designed as a landplane), but the lack of usable airstrips at that time made operating a seaplane more practical; the Merkur was more than suitable, since all the destinations were next to the shore. Having been redesigned to operate off floats, it thus had a higher overall profile than the Wal. This higher profile meant that landing the aircraft at night was more difficult. An effective solution to this, devised by the crew, was to fix a lead weight on the end of a rope several metres below the aircraft. Once the lead weight had touched the water, the pilot knew it was safe to land, because a blue light would appear on the instrument panel. After further checking that there were no obstructions, such as tree trunks or canoes on the lagoon, they would then land.

Named *Gaúcho* (*Cowboy*), in honour of the people from Rio Grande do Sul, the Merkur operated between different towns than the Wal, and connected the Atlantic coastal towns of Cidreira, Tramandaí and Torres, located in the north of the state, with Porto Alegre. It was registered P-BAAB, entered service on 24 November and remained in the fleet until 1930, when both it and the Wal were disposed of. However, *Gaúcho* had suffered structural damage, and, in December 1927, the insurers insisted that it had to be retired.

With a finite life in sight for the seaplanes, Meyer decided to buy two Klemm L 25s to replace them. This was an unusual choice, as the Klemm only had seating for one passenger. The aircraft were delivered in 1929 and primarily used for carrying mail and occasional training. In 1931, two further aircraft were acquired. This time, Meyer opted for the Junkers A50, a twin-seat monoplane, similar to the Klemm. Operations were largely confined to cargo and mail, and the aircraft were used occasionally for banner-towing. Both the Klemm and the Junkers were landplanes, and by this time, small airstrips had been opened up and were now being used for the operation. This enabled the aircraft to fly into the interior of the state and the A50s were used for this purpose. Later, these aircraft were used for training until 1944, when they were retired from service.

In 1930, a revolution took place in several states in Brazil, which included Rio Grande do Sul. It was caused largely by economic turmoil following a drop in the price of coffee. There was little business activity in the area during this time, and one of the L 25s had crashed on 30 September 1930, leaving the airline with only the remaining Klemm, and, indeed, at one point, all services had been suspended. The aftermath of the revolution brought about a significant loss of revenue, and this put Varig in dire financial straits by the end of 1931.

The Dornier Merkur, named *Gaúcho*, was the second aircraft to go onto the Brazilian register. (Varig.com)

Varig then acquired two small aircraft: a Morane-Saulnier MS.130, a small high-winged monoplane, effectively no more than a trainer, and a Nieuport-Delage (NiD) 641, a six-seat cabin monoplane. On 18 January 1931, another Junkers A50 Junior, P-BAAE, also joined the fleet. This aircraft was used to open a new route between Porto Alegre and Santa Maria, with a stop in Santa Cruz. However, misfortune befell Varig again. In April, the A50 crashed after only three months with the airline. Following this, a complete reorganisation of the airline took place, and the state of Rio Grande do Sul state lent Varig the money to buy two new Junkers F 13s from Germany. This aircraft was a low-wing monoplane capable of carrying five passengers and was the world's first all-metal transport aircraft. The nomenclature for registrations had now been changed, and these aircraft were registered as PP-VAF and PP-VAG. PP-VAF was named *Livramento* and PP-VAG *Santa Cruz* respectively, reflecting the names of the interior towns to which they operated. The first flight took place on 18 April 1932. New routes within Rio Grande do Sul were added, and a further two A50s were received during 1932, but one was quickly written off.

Flying at this time was extremely rudimentary. There were no toilets on board and no catering. For the pilots, navigation was done with the assistance of a compass and a pocket watch, though as the names of railway stations were painted on the roofs, these were used as additional navigation aids. One pilot, Captain Franz Greiss, apparently used very unconventional techniques when flying in poor weather conditions. He would put his head out of the window to smell the air. If he could small coal dust, then he knew he was over the coal-mining area of Arroio dos Ratos in Rio Grande do Sul. On flights to Uruguay, he would see pastures with cattle. He then knew that the landing strip was not far away, because the cattle were not disturbed by the noise of the aircraft. At that time, airfields were little more than cleared strips with few or no facilities. Much of the countryside was unpopulated at this time; huge areas of featureless grassland would suddenly give way to dense jungle. Rivers were of little help; the geology of the country was such that each tributary of a river looked much like another. Only on the coastlines were there definable landmarks or basic navigational aids. Turbulence was a regular factor. In a state only slightly smaller than Italy, wildly varying weather conditions were to be expected and, for the first time, seat belts were fitted.

The use of German aircraft to operate its services continued when, in the autumn of 1936, the Messerschmitt Bf 108B Taifun (Typhoon) was introduced for a brief period. The aircraft was originally designed as a four-seat recreation aircraft and incorporated new innovations, such as a retractable undercarriage, and was, in fact, the predecessor to the Bf 109 fighter. Following the new nomenclature, this aircraft was assigned the registration PP-VAJ. This, too, was written off some months later. One further German aircraft, this time a Messerschmitt M.20b, a ten-seat high-winged single-engined passenger aircraft, was added to the fleet and flew its first revenue service on 30 April 1937. This enabled the route network to reach Uruguaiana, a town in the west of Rio Grande do Sul on the Argentinian border.

Varig took the opportunity to buy a Junkers Ju 52/3mge, formerly owned by South African Airways, which was delivered on 10 March 1938. However, it only flew when there were sufficient numbers to make the flight economically viable. Since it had 17 seats, it was considerably larger than anything the company had operated previously. It did not formally enter service until 6 July and was named *Mauá*, after a town in Sao Paulo state. It was registered PP-VAL and used to open a new route from Porto Alegre to the coastal resort of Torres in the north of the state. However, an improvement in the roads linking the two towns meant that the service operated for only one season. In an unfortunate twist of fate, this aircraft crashed into the River Guaíba after taking off from Porto Alegre on 28 February 1942, killing six of its 21 occupants.

Two further German aircraft were acquired, this time two Focke-Wulf Fw 58s, leased from Condor. Varig preferred European aircraft, but, aware of war brewing in Europe and its current German connections, the company was worried the Allies could restrict supplies for parts and equipment, so the Italian Fiat G.2 was chosen to replace its Ju 52. The G.2 was, in fact, a rare type, as only a few had been built. They had been specifically designed for Bruno Mussolini, the son of Italian dictator Benito Mussolini. The aircraft were now being named after rivers, and this one became *Jacui*.

The effects of World War Two were, initially, less noticeable in Brazil than in many other countries, and the expansion of air services continued unabated. Nevertheless, it became apparent that the war with Germany would mean that operations would become more difficult, especially in terms of fuel and replacement parts, and because it had a German manager-director. For this reason, Otto Ernst Meyer resigned on 24 December 1941, and the shareholders decided that the next manager-director had to be a native-born Brazilian. A new name, Érico de Assis Brasil, appeared on the list of directors, but his tenure was to be short-lived, as following his appointment, he was killed in a tragic flying accident in November 1942, so the company had to look for a new leader.

In the early days of Varig, Ruben Martin Berta, a Brazilian-born son of German parents, and previously a medical student, had responded to an advertisement in a local newspaper in 1927, and, in fact, had become Meyer's first employee at the age of just 19. He had been a loyal employee throughout the early life of Varig, and, because of his background, Berta was voted onto the Varig board in 1943. However, the effects of World War Two were by now so widespread that the business had begun to decline, thus revenue was considerably reduced. Such was his love for the airline that Berta, a keen philatelist, sold his valuable stamp collection in order to keep Varig flying during this time.

An important day in the Varig calendar, 5 August 1942, marked the opening of the first international route from Porto Alegre to Montevideo, Uruguay. It is perhaps surprising to recall that, until this date, despite having existed for 15 years, none of Varig's flights had operated out of its home state of Rio Grande do Sul. It would be 1946 before services to other Brazilian states commenced. The Fiat G.2, PP-VAM, was used to inaugurate the service, but later a de Havilland 89 Dragon Rapide, fitted with six seats, was used for the twice-weekly operation. It carried the registration PP-VAN during its life with Varig and was later sold on to Organização Mineira de Transportes Aéreo (OMTA) as PP-OMA and was broken up in the 1950s at Belo Horizonte. The aircraft, which sits in the Museu Aeroespacial in Rio de Janeiro, was formerly registered to the Angola Aero Club with the Portuguese colonial registration CR-LKR and was disassembled and brought to Brazil for exhibition.

Chapter 2

Local Expansion, 1945–65

With the aim of providing a foundation that would provide financial, health, and social benefits for its employees, Ruben Berta decided to transfer 50 per cent of the company's shareholding to its employees. This became known as the Fundação Ruben Berta (Ruben Berta Foundation, henceforth referred to as RBF).

With World War Two at an end, war surplus aircraft began to flood the market. Many new and existing airlines were quick to see the benefits of the DC-3, and Varig was no exception. With their tradition of having a diminutive name for their aircraft, the Brazilians soon began to call them 'Douglinhas.' They began operations on the newly extended routes in 1946, typically from Porto Alegre to São Paulo and on to Rio de Janeiro. They were also used on the international route to Montevideo, which later continued to Buenos Aires. This flight was initially performed by a C-46 Commando, with the first flight taking off from Rio on 30 June 1952 and calling at Sao Paulo, Porto Alegre and Montevideo en route. The flight operated three times a week and took about seven and a half hours.

It was not only Varig that was expanding. The availability of cheap aircraft meant that new airlines were appearing in many different areas of Brazil, many in the northeast. A typical example was Aero Geral, based in Natal, in the northeast of Brazil. In May 1952, Varig bought Aero Geral, which previously operated five PBY-5 Catalinas along the Amazon, owned a lone C-46 Commando and

The C-46 played an important part in opening up Brazil's interior. (Bob O'Brien collection)

Seen here in the early days of Congonhas, one of Varig's many C-46-D-15-CUs. (Stefano Pagiola)

two DC-3s, but the interest was less in the aircraft it operated, and more in the route network. This marked a new departure for Varig because Aero Geral operated regular flights between Natal and Santos. The plan was to link the routes of the two airlines, thus providing a continuous service from the south to the north of the country along the east coast. The end of World War Two had seen increasing prosperity in Brazil, and having taken the opportunity to expand its operations as far north as Natal, Varig then found itself in direct competition with two other established carriers, Panair do Brasil, which had begun operations in October 1929 and Cruzeiro do Sul, which had begun life as Condor Syndikat, but was renamed in 1943. Both airlines were headquartered in Rio de Janeiro.

One way to deal with this, in Berta's view, was to expand the route network, and on 2 May 1961, Varig bought into another operator, the São Paulo-based Real Transportes Aéreos. Real had been a major competitor of Varig's for many years, operating successfully on similar routes, so the move was purely strategic. Prior to the Varig takeover, Real had itself purchased the already-established Aerovias Brasil, also based in São Paulo, thus strengthening its own network. This combined company became known as Consórcio Real Aerovias. The Aerovias route network was centred around the Rio de Janeiro–São Paulo–Belo Horizonte triangle, which was rapidly becoming the commercial hub of the country, and since the carrier operated DC-3s and C-46s, they fitted neatly into Varig's existing fleet. The third member of this consortium, Nacional, had also been purchased by Real prior to the Varig takeover and was included in the deal. Like Real, Nacional was based in São Paulo, but in addition to operating into Belo Horizonte, it also had routes to Cuiabá in the centre of Brazil and Salvador on the northeast coast. As with Aerovias and Real, it also operated DC-3s and C-46s. However, Real had run into severe financial problems and, as a result, sold half of its shares to Varig. On 16 August 1961, Real sold its remaining shares to Varig, thus completing the takeover. The first car-manufacturing facility in São Paulo was established in 1957, meaning that Brazilians could purchase a car without having to pay a punitive import tax and were now able to move about more freely and more economically. This had

PP-ITE operated with a number of Brazilian operators before joining Varig. (Helio Bastos Salmon)

contributed in some measure to the downfall of Real. With the takeover of Real complete, the number of cities served on Varig's domestic network had grown to more than 90, and its fleet consisted of almost 100 aircraft.

With these acquisitions, Varig now had 47 DC-3s in its fleet, but in the late 1950s the company began to slowly retire them and, by the end of the 1960s, they were being used mainly for cargo, or operating routes in the southern states of Rio Grande do Sul and Santa Catarina. However, it was 1971 before the last aircraft left the fleet. One other aircraft that Varig operated in large numbers during this period was the C-46 Commando. The Real purchase meant that its C-46 fleet had doubled. Others had been acquired during the takeover of Aero Geral. The C-46 was particularly useful, being as agile on unpaved surfaces as the DC-3, but with the advantage of being able to carry more passengers and cargo. They were operated in three configurations: luxury with 32 seats in a 2+2 seating configuration with wide seats; the combi version would be fitted with 46 seats in a 2+3 configuration; and it operated as an all-cargo variant as well.

The C-46 was known for having poor single-engine performance, being somewhat underpowered. In order to improve its performance, some were fitted with a small Turbomeca Palas turbojet located under the wing. The work was carried out by L. B. Smith Aircraft Corporation in Miami prior to operation with Varig. Some aircraft were also fitted with electrically actuated constant speed three- and four-bladed propellers and more powerful versions of the Pratt & Whitney Double Wasp engine. These were known as Super C-46Cs. In cargo configuration, the C-46 could carry five tonnes of cargo compared with four tonnes on the DC-3. Varig operated no less than 54 C-46s, some bought from the market, and others joining the fleet through Varig's acquisition of other carriers. The C-46 formed part of the Varig fleet between 1948 and 1970.

The next aircraft to be purchased by Varig was the Convair 240. Unlike the DC-3 and C-46, this aircraft had been specifically designed for the civil aviation market. Its pressurised cabin was less noisy and enabled the aircraft to fly at higher altitudes, making it much easier to avoid turbulence. Perhaps more importantly, to Varig at least, was the fact that it could fly at faster speeds than either the DC-3 or

A typical example of a DC-3 in Varig's colours. (Vito Cedrini)

C-46, with a cruising speed of 280mph (450km/h), compared to the DC-3 at 207mph (333km/h), and the C-46 at 173mph (278km/h). This was an important consideration in a country as large as Brazil, often with long sectors en route. Deliveries of the Convairs, most of which had previously served with Pan American (Pan Am), began in 1954 and continued until 1959. These were registered PP-VCK, PP-VCN to VCR, then VCV to VCZ. The remaining aircraft were registered PP-VDG and VDH. Further Convairs, this time the more modern and powerful versions of the aircraft, known as the Convair 340 and 440, were added to the fleet in 1961, following the takeover of Real Aerovias.

In total, three Convair 340s and nine 440s were added to the fleet. The Convair 340 was a lengthened version of the Convair 240, which enabled the addition of four seats. In addition, it had an extended wingspan to enable better performance at airfields with higher elevations. The final piston-engined version, the 440, also known as the Metropolitan, was a step up from the 340, with an elongated cabin that could accommodate up to 53 passengers, although in Varig service, the aircraft would be fitted with 40 seats. It took over the routes from both the DC-3 and the C-46, including both the domestic and international services. It was also the first aircraft to operate on what was by then becoming recognised as the Air Bridge between Rio and São Paulo. Although Varig had begun its life in Porto Alegre, and this was the maintenance centre for the airline, the main runway there was still unpaved, and it was not until 1954 that a Convair 240 became the first aircraft to land on the newly paved runway. All the Convair 340s and 440s were in operation by 1961, but none were kept in operation beyond 1963, although the 240s were kept in operation until 1970.

Whilst route expansion was taking place on the domestic flights, the international routes were not being ignored. In February 1953, the Brazilian government awarded the New York route to Varig. The airline placed an order for three Lockheed L-1049G Super Constellations and decided, as part of the launch of this prestigious new route, to provide a superior onboard service. For the first time, Varig took on female flight attendants – only men had been employed in this role previously. However, with reclining seats fitted in first class, it was not considered proper to have men attending to women and children who were preparing to sleep on the seats. The level of comfort and onboard service offered on the Super G Constellation flights had not previously been achieved. They were fitted with 15 tourist

After leaving Varig service, this aircraft flew with a number of other Brazilian airlines. (Vito Cedrini)

This aircraft was placed on display at the former Varig site, but then destroyed following Varig's bankruptcy on 31 January 2020. (Stefano Pagiola)

This aircraft went on to Venezuela and Nicaragua after leaving Varig, but it was destroyed during Hurricane Andrew in August 1992. (Helio Bastos Salmon)

An example of the Convair 240 at Santos Dumont Airport in Rio. (Helio Bastos Salmon)

A little line maintenance is carried out at Santos Dumont, Rio's downtown airport. (Stefano Pagiola Collection)

class seats at the front of the aircraft; these were in five rows with three sets on one side and two on the other. Behind those were two toilets, and then 28 first class seats arranged in seven rows, two by two. Behind this, there was a lounge with rotating seats and a further 11 first class seats. Meals were of a high standard too, with catering being overseen by a chef who had once worked for the Russian royal family. This marked the beginning of a superior onboard service for which Varig became famous, and which lasted until the final days of the airline. The level of service offered may seem rather indulgent by today's standards, but in the 1950s, long-haul flying was mainly undertaken only by the wealthy, who were prepared to pay a premium for, and expected, such luxury.

Initially, the order had been placed for the L-1049 'E' version, but this was amended. Real, which was also operating on the route, had acquired the 'H' version, which, to many, suggested that the Real aircraft was more modern than the 'G' version. However, the 'H' suffix simply meant that it could easily be adapted from carrying passengers to carrying cargo. Varig was rather haunted by this letter suffix, so when three further L-1049Gs arrived in 1957, it decided to paint the wingtip tanks fitted to this version with the words 'Super Intercontinental', with the letter 'I' being painted in large letters. The four aircraft that Real had used on these flights were operated for a while longer following Varig's takeover in 1961, but they were later converted for cargo use, and finally disposed of in 1969.

On 2 August 1955, the inaugural flight to New York took place, with technical stops at Belem and Ciudad Trujillo in the Dominican Republic. The service operated three times a week and offered connections to Buenos Aires and Montevideo, in addition to other cities in Brazil. Varig was competing with Pan American on the route. With its wide-ranging domestic and short-haul international routes in place, Varig was able to offer numerous connections to these flights, something Pan Am was unable to do, thus improving the load factor. In November 1955, Varig was granted a subsidy for the route, which had now been extended to four times a week and included Port-of-Spain (Trinidad), as

Another photo from Santos Dumont, where this aircraft is being prepared for the Air Bridge. (Helio Bastos Salmon)

an alternative to Belem. However, the loss of one of the L-1049Gs (PP-VDA) in Ciudad Trujillo on 16 August 1957 following an engine failure, meant that the US flights had to be reduced to thrice-weekly once more.

Prior to the takeover by Varig, Real had also begun operations in 1958 with a different version of the Super Constellation, the L-1049H, on a route from Rio de Janeiro to Los Angeles, via Manaus, Bogotá and Mexico City. In 1960, this route was extended to Honolulu and on to Tokyo. The entire flight from São Paulo to Tokyo would take a week. In a further addition to the long-haul fleet, the absorption of Real had provided Varig with five DC-6B aircraft. All had originally been bought from the used market, with PP-YSI, YSJ and YSL previously serving with Scandinavian Airlines System. PP-YSM and YSN had been bought directly from Northwest Airlines in the US. They were used principally on roues to the south, while the Super G Constellations in the fleet were used on the northern routes. The DC-6s proved popular with passengers, being faster than their predecessors and able to offer a considerable improvement in comfort. Whilst some operators had fitted 102 seats in their aircraft, Varig, with the emphasis as ever on comfort and service, only fitted 80 seats. All five aircraft were transferred to the Brazilian Air Force in 1968, after their seven-year service with Varig.

Two more propeller-driven aircraft had an important part to play in the development of Varig. The first was the Electra Mk II, an aircraft which Varig almost did not operate, but which became a huge favourite with its passengers. The Brazilian Directorate for Civil Aviation had become aware that a number of accidents had occurred with aircraft on the Rio–São Paulo Air Bridge and, as a result of this, issued a decree in 1975 that only four-engined aircraft could be used on the route. Whilst Varig had previously used an assortment of twin-engined aircraft on the route, VASP, the São Paulo-based participant in the Air Bridge, had been using the Japanese-built YS-11 together with Convair 240s, 340s, 440s and DC-3s.

Looking rather weather beaten, PP-VDG sits outside at the Bebeduoro Museum in São Paulo. (Marco Aurelio)

When Varig took over Real, it was unaware that Real had made a deal with American Airlines (AA) to purchase four Electras. News of this reached Varig's president, Ruben Berta, who was aware of the poor safety record of the Electra at the time, and he immediately took the next flight to the US to try to abort the deal. However, AA refused to cancel the contract, and Varig was forced to take delivery of the aircraft. Airlines typically plan their fleet acquisitions two years in advance, and the arrival of these unwanted aircraft posed a problem for Varig. Which routes could it operate them on? The first Electra arrived in Brazil on 30 August 1962, followed by the remaining three later that year. Initially, they were used on the longer-haul Brazilian domestic services, for example to Recife and Manaus, but later they were used on the routes to South American capitals. The limited range of the Electra II meant that refuelling stops were required, and the routes to Asunción, Montevideo and Buenos Aires were perfect for this. They were also used briefly on the 'Friendship Flights' linking Rio and Lisbon, the first of which took place on 22 November 1965. For this flight, technical stops were made in Recife and the island of Sal in the Cabo Verde Islands and, given the lack of navigational aids at the time, a navigator was also carried. In early 1963, following the edict issued by the Civil Aviation Directorate regarding four-engined operations on the Air Bridge, VASP had begun to use its Vickers Viscounts, many of them acquired from British European Airways during 1962 and 1963. In order to compete with VASP, Varig began to use the Electras on the Air Bridge. Despite Varig's earlier misgivings, the Electras proved to be very dependable, although deeper maintenance could only be carried out in Porto Alegre and was often complicated and time-consuming.

Sitting alongside a number of other aircraft that had been withdrawn from service is Convair 240 PP-VCN. (Bob O'Brien Collection)

This is PP-VDG in much better condition, seen here at Santos Dumont. (Bob Garrard Collection)

This Convair 440, PP-YRG, was formerly owned by Real and was acquired when Varig took them over. (Stefano Pagiola)

Avro 748 Series 2 PP-VDV is prepared for the long flight to Brazil at the factory in Manchester. (David R Lawrence)

Below: PP-VDO was one of the 11 Avro 748s that Varig operated. (David R Lawrence)

The Avro 748 was used by Varig to open new routes throughout Brazil. (Helio Bastos Salmon)

This aircraft spent less than two years in Varig service before being written off in a landing accident in Uberlandia. (Lloyd Robinson)

Below: PP-VDX taxies in at Congonhas in this early photo of Sao Paulo's downtown airport. (Stefano Pagiola Collection)

PP-PDO taxies in at Santos Dumont. Note the word 'Avro' to the right of the forward door and over the passenger door. (Bob O'Brien)

Despite the difficult operating conditions, Varig's 748s were invariably immaculate. (Bob O'Brien)

An early view of Congonhas, as Avro 748 PP-VDX taxies in. (Stefano Pagiola Collection)

Varig operated two DC-6s, originally acquired after their takeover of Real. (Helio Bastos Salmon)

The DC-6B was probably one of biggest aircraft at Santos Dumont. (Helio Bastos Salmon)

Varig's competitor, Real, had the Super H Constellation, but Varig wanted to emphasise the 'I' because it then appeared to be a newer aircraft. (Helio Bastos Salmon)

Below: The Electras proved to be very popular with their passengers. Note the rear windows, indicating that this aircraft had a lounge at the back. (Helio Bastos Salmon)

Chapter 3

Brazil's Boom Years, Mid-1960s

In the space of 55 years between 1950 and 2005, the population of Brazil grew from about 51 to 187 million inhabitants, an increase of more than 2 per cent per year. Naturally, such an increase meant that the airlines had increasing numbers of passengers at their disposal.

The Air Bridge

With its large seats and comfortable interior, including a seven-seat lounge at the rear of some of the aircraft, the Electra quickly became popular with passengers. The fleet was operated in an all-economy configuration. In spite of its earlier misgivings with the aircraft, the carrier was encouraged to go back to the market, but by now sources for used Electras were beginning to dry up. Two further aircraft were sourced from Braniff International Airlines, but they differed from the previous aircraft in that they were equipped with large freight doors and thus capable of carrying cargo, which they were occasionally used for. Varig decided not to convert them, and both aircraft, PP-VLA and PP-VLB, remained throughout their Varig service with just the rear door operative. Their primary duty by this time, though, was to operate on the Air Bridge between Rio and Sao Paulo. The Electras began operations on that route in September 1962 and gave almost 30 years of continuous service until the last flight on 6 January 1992. The Air Bridge, during these years, was second only in intensity to the New York–Washington service, and the operation is worthy of further explanation.

The cities of Rio de Janeiro and São Paulo are situated a little more than 200 miles (320km) apart, but in real terms, they have little in common. Rio de Janeiro, with its famous beaches and landmarks,

An Electra operating the Air Bridge taxies onto the stand at Santos Dumont. (Author)

The close proximity of Sugarloaf Mountain to Santos Dumont is clearly visible. (Helio Bastos Salmon)

is known to the natives, called Cariocas, as 'a cidade marvilhosa' – 'the marvellous city'. The citizens of São Paulo, called Paulistas, see things rather differently. They consider the Cariocas to be lazy and hedonistic, and themselves to be energetic and hard-working. There are good reasons for this. While Rio was the capital from 1763 until 1960 and therefore the centre of diplomacy and banking, São Paulo grew rapidly during the 1960s through the trading of commodities, not least of which was coffee. There is a standing joke in Sao Paulo that the famous statue of Christ in Rio with its outstretched arms, will clap its hands when the Cariocas finally do some work. Despite the rivalries, the wheels of business and industry mean that frequent travel between the two cities is essential. However, it is not just business for which people travel. The only alternative to flying is to travel by road since there are no rail journeys available. Even today, a typical road journey can take five hours, with heavy traffic in evidence throughout the journey. The relatively low fares on the Air Bridge in the 1960s and later frequently attracted a lot of what is known in the airline industry as VFR traffic – visiting friends and relations. The current population of São Paulo city itself is 12 million and that of Rio is close to seven million, so there is ample opportunity for this. The fact that both airports used for the Air Bridge are less than 5 miles (8km) from the city centre, is an added attraction. However, the fact that they are city-centre airports naturally restricts their flying hours, with the first departures from either airport not permitted before 0600hrs, and the last departure at 2300hrs. During the time of the Electra operation, there would typically be 37 return flights during weekdays between the two cities, with 22 return flights at weekends. In addition to this, there would be 16 flights a day each way between Rio's Galeão and São Paulo's Congonhas airports, with a combination of Boeing 727s and 737s.

At the peak hours of the day during the week, there would be a flight every 15 minutes. Although the flight was primarily operated by Varig, the route was, in fact, a pool service operated in conjunction with VASP, Cruzeiro and TransBrasil, with revenues being split 52 per cent, 22 per cent, 19 per cent and 7 per cent, respectively. Tickets for the Air Bridge could be bought at any of the four operators, but reservations were not required. Initially, all the aircraft carried Varig titles, but the other three carriers complained that, since they were operating a pool service, their names should also be on the aircraft.

A busy apron scene at Congonhas Airport, São Paulo, in 1985. (Author)

Sometimes it rains in Rio! With umbrellas provided by the airport authority, the passengers make their way to the departing Electra. Air bridges have now been fitted to the terminal. (Author)

There was always a standby aircraft available during the Air Bridge operation, in case of unserviceability. (Author)

A compromise was reached in 1975, whereby four of the aircraft, PP-VJE, PP-VJN, PP-VJU and PP-VLC, had their Varig titles and logos removed, leaving just the Varig cheat line. However, this lack of identification confused the passengers and, in 1979, the full Varig logos were restored. Buoyed by the success of the Air Bridge, Varig purchased a further Electra in November 1976 and a final aircraft in 1986. Varig operated a total of 15 Electras. One aircraft was written off in a landing accident at Porto Alegre on 5 February 1970, but, fortunately, there were only minor injuries. The Air Bridge was generally a very smooth operation, and even a major fire that almost destroyed the terminal building at Rio's Santos Dumont airport in 1999 did not hamper the operation. For the six months during which the terminal was rebuilt, an airport hangar was used for processing Air Bridge passengers.

Inevitably and reluctantly, a decision had to be taken to replace the Electras. After a number of evaluations, including the Fokker 100 and the BAe 146, the Boeing 737-300 was chosen and the final flight with the Electra took place on 6 January 1992. The aircraft which performed it, PP-VJM, made a farewell flight around Rio de Janeiro, which was televised live, before being retired to the Museu Aeroespacial in Campo dos Afonsos near the city.

The second propeller-driven aircraft to achieve legendary status within Varig was the Hawker Siddeley 748, known locally as the 'Avro'. The airline needed a DC-3 replacement and studied a number of alternative aircraft that were being offered as potential DC-3 replacements. Many airfields in Brazil, particularly in the interior, were still not fully developed, had short unpaved runways and very limited navigation and air traffic control facilities. In December 1965, an Avro 748 was leased to Varig for almost a year and was registered as PP-VDQ. The first flight operated by the aircraft was between São Paulo and Iguaçu Falls on 23 December 1965, and such was the reliability of the 748 on the subsequent schedules that they often operated up to ten sectors per day, with turnarounds being as short as ten minutes at some of the more remote jungle strips. As a result of this, the airline decided on the aircraft, not least because of its demonstrable ability to operate from unpaved airfields. The first of ten aircraft, PP-VDN, was delivered on 14 November 1967, with the final aircraft, PP-VDX (PP-VDW was not allocated), being received on 15 September 1968. The complete batch was delivered as Series 2 aircraft, but were later converted to Series 2As, which offered improved performance. In 1970, the aircraft were used to operate flights under the title of Rede de Integração Nacional (National Integration Network). This network was put in place to open routes to smaller towns in the interior,

These two aircraft, PP-VLA and VLB, seen here at Congonhas, were bought from Northwest Airlines and were fitted with large freight doors, so only the rear door is operative. (Author)

some of which had previously been operated by the DC-3s and others which had not been operated previously. They were also used frequently on the Air Bridge.

The rapid growth of air travel in Brazil during this period brought about the significant upgrading of many airfields, and thus an increase in passengers. The Avro 748, now a victim of its own success, was no longer able to offer the capacity required on many routes and was replaced by jets. By September 1975, the first of the aircraft had been sold off to Bouraq of Indonesia and the last aircraft left service in January 1977.

The other turboprop that Varig operated were four Fairchild Hiller FH-227Bs, PP-BUG–BUJ, which had been brought into the fleet following the bankruptcy of Paraense, an operator based in Belém in the northeast of the country. The aircraft had been taken on charge by the Ministry of Aeronautics and then leased to Varig after Paraense had ceased operations on 30 May 1970. The Brazilian government had withdrawn Paraense's operating certificate following the crash of an FH-227 in the previous March. The aircraft was manufactured as a US version of the F-27, as licensed by Fokker, but with a longer fuselage than the F-27, enabling it to carry 56 passengers, a radome to accommodate weather radar and additional fuel capacity. They were mainly used as supplemental aircraft on the Air Bridge and were painted with the Varig cheat line but did not carry the Varig logo or titles. The declaration by the Directorate General of Civil Aviation about only using four-engined aircraft on the Air Bridge meant that they were withdrawn from the route soon afterwards. Varig's habit of nicknaming their aircraft continued with the FH-227. It became known as 'Boko-Moko', a phrase basically meaning outdated, after a character in a beer commercial. The aircraft stayed in the fleet for just five years, with two aircraft, PP-BUG and -BUJ being sold to TABA, a third-level carrier based in Belém and operating services along the Amazon. The remaining two aircraft were sold to Aerochaco in Argentina after being stored at São Paulo's Congonhas airport for several years.

One of the biggest shocks for Varig during this period was the sudden death of the airline's leader, Ruben Berta. On 14 December 1966, he was working at his office desk in Rio de Janeiro when he felt stabbing pains in his chest. A doctor was called, but Berta insisted on continuing to work. An hour later, he was dead. He had worked for Varig for 40 years, having joined the airline at the age of 19.

PP-VNK sits at Santos Dumont, awaiting passengers. This aircraft was written-off whilst firefighting in Canada on 16 July 2003. (Bob O'Brien Collection)

PP-VDE taxies in at what was then Idlewild Airport, now John F. Kennedy International Airport, in the days when Constellations ruled the skies. (Stefano Pagiola)

A Boeing 707-320C does a low pass over Jacarepaguá airfield during an airshow in Rio de Janeiro. (Vito Cedrini)

One of the three Conway-engined Boeing 707s arrives at Galeão airport, Rio. There is no explanation for the pod on the No 2 engine. (Helio Bastos Salmon)

PP-VJY is a Boeing 707-345 series with a large freight door. This series had the Pratt & Whitney JT3D engines. (Richard Vandervord)

Sadly, PP-VJK was written off following an engine failure on take-off from Abidjan on 3 January 1987. (Bob O'Brien Collection)

This aircraft spent 18 years in service with Varig before being sold to the Brazilian Air Force. (Helio Bastos Salmon)

The cargo door arrangement can be clearly seen in this photo. Seventeen of Varig's Boeing 707s were fitted in this way. (Bob O'Brien Collection)

A photo from the long-ago days of Heathrow, showing PP-VJR. This aircraft was destroyed in a hangar fire at Galeão on 7 September 1968. (Gerry Manning)

PP-VJX was on Varig's books for 18 years before being converted to a tanker for the Brazilian Air Force. (Bob O'Brien)

PP-VLM carries the Varig Cargo titles. This aircraft was originally owned by Continental Airlines. (Richard Vandervord)

This was the first Boeing 707 delivered to Varig, and it also spent a brief lease period with British Overseas Airways Corporation (BOAC). (Richard Vandervord)

Another photo of the ill-fated PP-VJK, taken at the cargo centre in Miami. (Richard Vandervord)

A busy scene at Idlewild as PP-VJA prepares to leave for Rio. (Gerry Manning)

Varig operated three Caravelles. This aircraft caught fire after running off the runway in Brasilia on 27 September 1961. (Bob O'Brien Collection)

PP-PDS joined the fleet following the demise of Panair do Brasil. It was one of two DC-8-33s in the fleet. (Helio Bastos Salmon)

This was one of three CV-990s operated by Varig, but they were not originally ordered by the airline. (Bob O'Brien Collection)

The Boeing 727 was a workhorse for Varig. PP-VLG is seen here at Curitiba before it was converted to a cargo version. (Author)

One of 12 Boeing 727-100 series, PP-VLR taxies onto the stand at Galeão.

PP-VLE has already been converted to a cargo version in this photo, taken at Congonhas. (Vito Cedrini)

This aircraft was one of several purchased from Delta Air Lines. (Helio Bastos Salmon)

Another photo of PP-VLE, this time at Curitiba. (Author)

The Boeing 727s were used on international as well as domestic routes. (Bob O'Brien Collection)

The new Varig logo has been applied to this Boeing 737-200 series, seen here at Galeão. This aircraft has been preserved and may be turned into an aviation-themed hotel. (Vito Cedrini)

The same aircraft in the original Varig scheme.

A busy scene at Santos Dumont during a turnround. Note the large bridge in the background. (Bob O'Brien Collection)

Below: Another busy scene, with Sugarloaf Mountain in the background, emphasising the limitations at Santos Dumont. (Richard Vandervord)

A former Rio-Sul aircraft, this Boeing 737-700 carries the legend 'We will go further for you' under the cabin windows. (Stefano Pagiola)

A distinctive colour scheme has been applied to this Boeing 737-300 to celebrate Brazil's fourth World Cup win in football in 1992. (Bob O'Brien)

PP-VQB is one of several Boeing 737-700s that were stored at Lasham airfield in the UK in 2002. (Richard Vandervord)

Another of the returned-from-lease aircraft at Lasham. All aircraft are Boeing 737-700 series. (Richard Vandervord)

Below: PP-VQE together with its stablemates at Lasham. (Richard Vandervord)

A former Tarom aircraft, this Boeing 737-300 was returned to the lessor after Varig was declared bankrupt. (Gerry Manning)

PP-VPS waits for its next load of passengers at Santos Dumont. This Boeing 737-300 series was returned to the lessor in 2002. (Bob O'Brien Collection)

Below: Boeing 737-300 PP-VOT carried out the inaugural jet service on the Rio–São Paulo Air Bridge, replacing the Electras. (Bob O'Brien Collection)

Chapter 4

Ushering in the Jet Era, The 1970s

Erik de Carvalho, who had taken over from Ruben Berta, was the president of Varig between December 1966 and March 1980. During this time, he oversaw the purchase of a number of interests that were only indirectly connected to Varig, one of which was Rotatur. Rotatur was a small charter airline and travel agency. The idea behind this was to provide tourist traffic for Varig's services. In 2003, the administrative board of Varig decided to discontinue the domestic operations of Rotatur and create the Varig Travel agency. He also bought Agropecuaria, an agricultural enterprise based in the state of Maranhão in northeastern Brazil. Agropecuaria consisted of 45,000 acres (18,210 hectares) of prime farmland, set up to produce livestock and general farming. Additionally, following the example of Pan Am and its founding of the Intercontinental Hotel chain, he set up a company called Tropical Hotels, which had four-star hotels in major tourist cities around Brazil, all of which were served by Varig.

Following a demonstration in Porto Alegre in April 1957, Varig placed an order for the first jet-powered aircraft to join the fleet. This was the Sud Aviation Caravelle. Originally built as Mk 1s, they were converted to Mk 3 standard in 1961. Varig was only the third airline in the world to order the aircraft, following Air France and Scandinavian Airlines System. PP-VJC, the first of three aircraft, was

PP-VMD was one of 15 DC-10-30s to be operated by Varig. (Vito Cedrini)

delivered to Porto Alegre on 16 September 1959 and, following a familiarisation period, was put into service the following month. The Caravelle had been bought to operate the longer principal domestic routes, such as Manaus, Recife and Belem. Varig had placed an order with Boeing for the new 707, but such was the demand for the ground-breaking jet, that delivery slots were protracted. Owing to this, the Caravelle was put into service to operate the Rio–New York route, with PP-VJC operating the first flight on 12 December 1959. Varig can claim to be the first airline to operate a jet into what then was Idlewild Airport, later renamed as John F. Kennedy International Airport. Given that the Caravelle was not designed for long-haul operations, a number of stops were necessary. The full operation began in Porto Alegre, with stops in Congonhas, Belém, Port-of-Spain, Nassau, and finally New York. On 20 January 1960, Brasilia was added to the route, prior to its inauguration as the new capital. There were now five flights a week on the route, three operated by the L-1049s and two by the Caravelles.

One redeeming feature for the passengers on such a long flight was the fact that the seating configuration was 2+2, with a total of 40 seats. Additionally, the Caravelle reduced the flight time previously set by the Super G Constellations from 25 hours to 14 hours. A second Caravelle, PP-VJD, was put into service on 12 December 1959. During these operations, on 27 September 1961, PP-VJD was involved in a landing accident in Brasilia. No passengers or crew were injured, but the aircraft was a write-off and Varig had to purchase a replacement aircraft from Air Algerie. This aircraft, PP-VJI, was delivered in December 1961, but stayed in the fleet for less than two years because it was becoming increasingly clear to Varig that, despite its popularity with passengers, the Caravelle did not easily fit into its current network. Once the final Boeing 707s had been delivered, the Caravelles were returned to domestic duties and a few short-haul international flights. With this in mind, the interiors were reconfigured, first with 52, then 68 and, finally, 73 seats, but after just five years of service, they were sold. PP-VJC was sold to Air Vietnam in August 1964 and PP-VJI, the former Air Algerie aircraft, went to Avensa in Venezuela in November 1964. The last scheduled flight took place in November 1963. One unusual aspect of the Caravelle's operation was that it could deploy a parachute to slow it down on landing. This is not uncommon on military aircraft, but the operation of the parachute then requires that it must be released after landing and collected from the runway later, which can interfere with traffic at a busy airport. As part of the upgrade to a Mk 3, and to obviate the need for a parachute, reverse thrust capabilities were fitted to the Rolls-Royce Avon engines.

The first aircraft to be delivered in this batch was PP-VMA. (Bob O'Brien Collection)

Originally delivered as a passenger aircraft, PP-VMT was later converted for cargo. (Richard Vandervord)

The Caravelles were replaced by a combination of Convair 990s, DC-6s and Electras, depending on the route. The arrival of the jets naturally reduced flight times, but many regional airports were still not suitably equipped to handle them. Using the acronym SITAR, the Brazilian aviation authority, in an effort to improve conditions, split the country into five regions, with each region having its own dedicated airline. Varig joined forces with a company called Top Taxi Aéreo, based in Teresina in the northeastern state of Piauí. Another carrier, Rio-Sul Servicios Aéreos Regionais, would serve the southern region, together with Espírito Santo, Rio de Janeiro and São Paulo. On 25 August 1976, the first flights within the southern states took place, using two Embraer 110 Bandeirantes in the colours of Rio-Sul.

The next jet aircraft to join the Varig fleet was the Convair 990 Coronado. In fact, Varig had not ordered these aircraft, but had acquired them following the take-over of Real, which ordered them in 1960. The aircraft, PP-VJE, VJF and VJG, were not received until 1963. In a clear case of déjà vu, relating to the purchase of the Electras, Varig tried to cancel the order, but was again unsuccessful. As part of its attempt to rescind the deal, Varig insisted that the CV 990 should be able to operate fully loaded out of Congonhas. At that time, the runway was a little over 5,000ft (1,524m) long, and Varig's lawyers had cited a clause in the contract between Convair and Real, which guaranteed that the CV 990 could take off from Congonhas at maximum take-off weight. Varig told Convair that it would only accept the aircraft if this could be proved. In response, Convair brought a CV 990 to Congonhas, filled it with sandbags to the maximum weight and the tests were carried out successfully.

Despite it being the world's fastest commercial airliner at the time, Varig never really took to the CV 990. Having just three aircraft of one type, with the attendant costs of maintenance, crew training and handling, increased operating restraints and costs significantly, so it was no surprise that they did not stay in the fleet for long. Having operated to Los Angeles and various destinations in South America and Europe, PP-VJE was withdrawn from the fleet in May 1967, after being sold to Alaska Airlines. The remaining two aircraft, PP-VJF and VJG, were withdrawn from service in 1971, with both aircraft going to Modern Air in the US in July of that year. Prior to this, Varig was the only airline in the world operating three different long-haul jet types, with Boeing 707s and a DC-8 also in the fleet.

PP-VMS undergoes a line check at Miami. (Michael Prophet)

The DC-8 was another aircraft which Varig acquired by default. After the apparent failure of Panair do Brasil in 1965, the airline was made to cease operations immediately, following an edict by the Brazilian military government, which had seized power the previous year. Its international routes were immediately transferred to Varig and, on the night of 15 February 1965, flight PB 22, due to operate Rio–Recife–Lisbon–Paris–Frankfurt was replaced by a Varig Boeing 707. On the following day, Panair do Brasil was declared bankrupt, with the government claiming an overseas debt of US$62m. A DC-8-33 and a DC-7C, both on lease from Pan American, were returned, and the remaining two DC-8s, PP-PDS and PP-PEA, were transferred to Varig. The fourth aircraft had been written off at Rio's Galeão airport in August 1962.

It is now believed that Varig was aware of the demise of Panair and thus had time to prepare for a takeover of its routes. It later became apparent that the shutdown of Panair was not because of financial problems, but political factors. The story that eventually emerged was that the new military government did not favour two of Panair's major shareholders, because they had been staunch supporters of the overthrown president and that this was simply an act of reprisal. The remaining assets of Panair were quickly disposed of and, by May 1966, all trace of the airline had disappeared. Of the two remaining aircraft, PP-PEA was written off whilst in Varig's colours during an approach to Monrovia airport in Liberia on 5 March 1967, while on a scheduled flight from Rome to Rio. PP-PDS remained as part of the fleet until 1978, when it was sold to American Jet Industries in the US.

The backbone of the long-haul fleet during this time was the Boeing 707. Varig had received the first three of these aircraft, designated series -441, in June 1960, directly from Boeing. These versions were powered by Rolls-Royce Conway engines. They began a non-stop service between Rio de Janeiro and New York on 22 June 1960, with Brasilia becoming a once-a-week stop on the service in July. However, the remainder of the fleet were in the -3xx series, all of which were powered by Pratt & Whitney JT-3D engines, which offered an increase in thrust, together with aerodynamic improvements, a higher fuel capacity and take-off weight, thus enabling them to fly non-stop between Rio de Janeiro and Europe. Following this, the -441 series were used mainly on flights to Miami, Los Angeles and the longer routes within South America. By 1965, Varig was operating 16 Boeing 707's, most of which were the -320C version.

The same aircraft at Heathrow. It was formerly with Singapore Airlines. (Richard Vandervord)

While the Boeing 707 was the mainstay of the long-haul fleet, it was the Boeing 727 that was charged initially with developing and improving the short haul routes. Four aircraft, all series 100s, were in the first batch, PP-VLD, VLF, VLG and VLH. The registration PP-VLE was not taken up initially and was later allocated to an aircraft bought from Antillean Airlines, which arrived with the second batch of aircraft in 1973. These aircraft were used to replace the Electras on some of the longer domestic routes and also within Latin America to destinations such as Bogotá, Mexico City and Caracas, with a final stop in Miami. Two further aircraft, PP-VLQ and VLR, were acquired from Delta Air Lines and added to the fleet in March 1973. A seventh aircraft, PP-VLD, joined the fleet from Airlift International the following month, followed by PP-VLS, ex-Japan Air Lines, and PP-VLT, formerly with Delta Air Lines, in 1974, bringing the total fleet to nine. All of these aircraft were -100 series.

The purchase of Cruzeiro do Sul in 1975 added another eight aircraft to the fleet, and two further 727s were acquired: PP-VLV, ex-Evergreen International, and an ex-Yemen Airways example, which became PP-VLW. The 727s proved equally useful as cargo aircraft and, in 1975, two aircraft were fully converted for this purpose. In October 1981, PP-VLR was sold to Saeta of Ecuador and, by October 1992, PP-VLF, VLH, VLQ, VLT and VLW had all been sold. PP-VLD, VLG and VLS were converted to all-cargo configuration and transferred to a Varig affiliate, known as VarigLog. Varig operated a total of 15 Boeing 727s, 11 of which were -100 series. The remaining four -200 series were also transferred to VarigLog.

As part of an overall fleet modernisation, Varig had ordered the Boeing 737-200, promoted as 'super advanced', and delivery of these enabled them to be incorporated into the fleet in 1974. The intention was for them to replace the 727-100s, although for some years both types operated alongside each other. The first of ten aircraft, PP-VME, was delivered in November 1974, followed by PP-VMF, VMG and VMH later that year. With these aircraft, Varig was able to fulfil the demand for seats throughout the country, brought about by an economic boom during this period. The remaining six aircraft, PP-VMI to VMN, were delivered during 1975.

On 4 June 1976, Varig's ambitions were dealt a severe blow by the government. A severe balance of payments deficit had accumulated, which concerned the government enough for them to introduce an exit tax. This meant that any Brazilian travelling overseas had to deposit 12,000 cruzeiros (more than US$800) with the Bank of Brazil. As if this were not penalty enough, the deposit had to be left with the bank for a year, with no interest payable to the depositor. This figure was raised to 16,000 cruzeiros

One of the batch of original DC-10-30s, PP-VMB is seen here at Heathrow. (Richard Vandervord)

(US$902) in February 1977. Inflation was in double digits at the time, so anyone who had to use the system faced an additional financial penalty by losing up to a quarter of the money they had originally deposited. The exit tax was not applicable for travel to some neighbouring countries, such as Argentina, Chile, Paraguay and Uruguay.

Initially, the Boeing 737s replaced the Electras on domestic services, thus freeing up the Electras to operate exclusively on the Air Bridge. Later, they also took over the domestic routes formerly operated by the Avro 748s. The first international route operated by the 737s was to Paraguay's capital, Asunción. A further six aircraft joined the Varig fleet in 1975, following its takeover of Cruzeiro, which until then had been a competitor. Varig now had 16 737s, but two further aircraft were acquired from Bavaria Fluggesellschaft in May 1982. In November 1996 and January 1997, a further two aircraft were leased from International Lease Finance Corporation, which meant that a total of 20 aircraft were operated, though these last two aircraft, originally registered as PP-VPD and VPE, were quickly transferred to Pluna Airlines of Uruguay, a company that was 49 per cent owned by Varig at that time. One good piece of news in these troubled times for the airline was that, in 1979, Varig was awarded 'Airline of the Year' for onboard quality, by the prestigious Air Transport World magazine.

In 1979, Boeing had begun to develop an improved version of the 737, to be known as the 737-300 and later as the 737 Classic. The intention was not only to maintain commonality with the 737-200, but also to incorporate numerous technological improvements. The new series offered increased capacity and range, together with the use of more fuel-efficient quieter engines that had come onto the market. For this, the CFM-56, a high by-pass turbofan engine produced under a French-American joint venture, had been chosen, which required a number of aerodynamic changes to be made to both the engine cowling and the wings. The first flight of the new series took place on 24 February 1984.

Soon after this, Varig placed an order, initially for four aircraft. The first of these was delivered in September 1987. In common with its tradition of having nicknames for its aircraft, Varig now named their 737-200s Brega (Tacky) and the 737-300s Chique (Chic), after two characters in one of the many Brazilian soap operas.

The -200 series remained in service until early 2002, and were about to be disposed of, when Varig ran into financial difficulties and had to reactivate four of them during the period August 2002 to June 2003. The identifying Varig cheat lines, title and logo had already been removed, and they operated with an all white scheme.

Another DC-10-30 that was converted to cargo is about to be pushed back at Heathrow. (Richard Vandervord)

Deliveries of the 737-300 eventually continued, with two further aircraft being delivered later in 1987 and being allocated in a block of registrations from PP-VNU–VNX. PP-VNW had been allocated to a leased Boeing 747. In late 1988, two further aircraft arrived and were allocated PP-VOD and VOE, with four more aircraft being delivered in 1989. By now, the total was 12 and there were more to come. In 1990, Varig received five more aircraft, plus eight more during the following year, thus making it the principal type in the fleet. In 1992, Varig began to replace the ageing Electras on the Air Bridge. However, this was not entirely successful, despite the flight time being 10 minutes shorter and the Boeing offering increased passenger capacity. To begin with, the parallel runways at Santos Dumont, the downtown airport in Rio de Janeiro used for the Air Bridge, are notoriously short at just 4,341ft (1,323m) and 4,240ft (1,260m), respectively. One of the runways had to be increased by 300m in order to enable a safe operation for the 737-300. Additionally, there are obstructions at both ends of the runways. A large, high bridge completely spanning Guanabara Bay sits to the north of the airfield and the Sugarloaf Mountain sits to the south. Also, being located near the Tropic of Capricorn, Rio de Janeiro can suffer from extreme weather events, and although the operation with the -300 was just about manageable, a heavy rain shower would require diversion to the main international airport – then known as Galeão, but renamed Antonio Carlos Jobim International Airport in January 1999, in honour of the composer of 'The Girl from Ipanema', and located 12 miles (20km) north of the city.

No further 737s were received until 1997, when five aircraft arrived during the year, in the sequence PP-VPQ–VPU. By this time, there were 34 737-300s in the fleet. Just a year later, with an eye to replacing the older -300s, Varig received its first Boeing 737-700, the first of five direct from Boeing, marketed as the New Generation (NG) aircraft series. The intention was to gradually retire the 737-300s, until Varig was engulfed in another fiscal crisis. Unable to order new 737-700NGs, the company reactivated the -300s and, by 2001, was operating 37 aircraft. All the aircraft were fully occupied on Brazil's domestic and some international flights, with some operating as far north as the Caribbean. The 737-300s remained in the Varig fleet until the carrier ceased operations in 2006.

While there was a lot of activity with flights and aircraft on the domestic scene, the long-haul was not being ignored. With one aircraft lost in Monrovia, the remaining DC-8 acquired from Panair do Brasil continued to operate until 1978. However, it was the Boeing 707s that were usually to be found in the Varig long-haul timetable. Three Rolls-Royce Conway-engined Boeings, designated series -420 were ordered, and the first of these had begun operations on 22 June 1960 on the Rio de Janeiro–New York

After service with Varig, this MD-11, PP-VOP, went to Gemini Air Cargo, after being converted to a cargo version. (Gerry Manning)

route. This was the longest scheduled flight in operation at the time, and the Boeings were frequently operating at maximum take-off weight. Because of this, they needed to make full use of the 13,123ft (4,000m) runway at Rio de Janeiro's Galeão airport, the longest runway in Brazil. Sometimes, the 707 was unable to gain sufficient height to stay safely above the downtown Santos Dumont airport, and it was necessary to delay movements there during the departure of this flight.

As the Boeing 707 was developed, Varig took a particular interest in the combi (part cargo, part passenger) version, known in Boeing configuration as the -341C. The combi version had a large freight door in the forward part of the fuselage, enabling bulky items of cargo to be loaded onto a specially adapted cabin floor. Passenger accommodation was at the rear of the aircraft. Despite the weight penalty incurred by the addition of the door, its mechanism and the reinforced floor, this arrangement proved particularly useful on routes where there was a lower passenger demand, but a significant cargo requirement. Additionally, the -341C had Pratt & Whitney engines installed, along with other aerodynamic improvements, a higher take-off weight and greater fuel capacity. This enabled the aircraft to operate non-stop to Europe from Rio de Janeiro. The first two aircraft, PP-VJR and VJS, arrived simultaneously on 28 December 1966, with a third aircraft, PP-VJT, arriving on 22 March 1967. Following the arrival of the combi aircraft, the original -420s were put into operation on the US routes.

In 1968, Varig received two more combi aircraft, which took the registrations PP-VJK and PP-VJX, followed by PP-VJH, VJY and VJZ the following year. Two further aircraft, PP-VLI and VLJ, were delivered in 1971, replacing the CV 990s, which by then had been taken out of service. Three more aircraft, PP-VLN, VLO and VLP, joined the fleet in 1973 and one final aircraft, PP-VLU, arrived in 1974.

This last aircraft became involved in what has become one of aviation's enduring mysteries. On 30 January 1979, it was operating flight RG 967, a scheduled all-cargo flight from Tokyo to Rio de Janeiro, with scheduled stops planned in Los Angeles and Lima. The aircraft was carrying 53 paintings belonging to the Japanese-Brazilian artist Manabu Mabe, which had been lent to Japan for an exhibition and were valued at US$1.25 million (US$5 million today). It had taken off from Tokyo's recently opened airport at Narita at 2023hrs and climbed in an east-north-easterly direction, to take the oceanic track towards Los Angeles, with the last contact being at 2045hrs. The flight was due to report to air traffic control at 2123hrs, but there was no contact. All emergency services were notified, including the Japanese Coast Guard, but no trace of the aircraft, its cargo, or its crew, has ever been found. This has led to various

A busy scene at the cargo terminal, as PP-VMT is loaded up. (Gerry Manning)

conspiracy theories being put forward, including the possibility of it having been shot down after straying into Russian airspace in the manner of Korean Air Lines flight KL 007 in 1983, but in reality, no conclusive explanation for the disappearance has been put forward. The aircraft was just five years old.

The -320 enabled Varig to open new routes to Asia and Africa, with Tokyo, Johannesburg and Luanda being added to the network. A route to Tokyo was inaugurated on 25 June 1968 and the Rio de Janeiro–Johannesburg–Luanda route was inaugurated on 21 August 1970. The flights to Japan proved to be particularly successful, since there is a large Japanese population in Brazil. As the widebody aircraft began to arrive, the fleet was gradually used on cargo-only services until 1989, when they were disposed of, with five of them joining the Brazilian Air Force as tanker aircraft.

PP-VMB was delivered to Varig on 18 June 1974. (Bob O'Brien Collection)

PP-VOQ also went to Gemini Air Cargo and was converted. (Bob O'Brien Collection)

This aircraft retained its registration when it was leased to Pluna of Uruguay in May 1999. (Gerry Manning)

PP-VPN had a relatively short life with Varig and was returned to the lessors in late 2003. (Gerry Manning)

Wearing the new Varig colour scheme, MD-11 PP-VQK later went to Táxi Aéreo Marília (TAM), and then to Ethiopian Airlines, where it was converted to a cargo aircraft. (Gerry Manning)

Brazil's fourth football World Cup win is celebrated on this MD-11, PP-VPP. (Gerry Manning)

The leasing company, Pegasus Aviation, had PR-LGD converted to a freighter, but it was only with VarigLog for three years. (Richard Vandervord)

Originally delivered in December 1993, PP-VPJ was sold to Boeing in 2005 and converted to a freighter. (Richard Vandervord)

PP-VPM followed the same path as VPJ and was converted to a freighter. (Richard Vandervord)

Another view of PP-VPP wearing its World Cup scheme. (Richard Vandervord)

After eight years' service with Varig, PP-VQK was leased to TAM until it went out of business. (Richard Vandervord)

After leaving Varig in 2000, PP-VOQ went to Gemini Air Cargo and was converted to a freighter. (Richard Vandervord)

PP-VMX was leased to Lineas Aéreas Paraguayas during its time with Varig. (Michael Prophet)

As with many of the Varig MD-11s, PP-VPL later became a freighter. (Richard Vandervord)

Another example of an MD-11 that was bought by Boeing in 2005 is PP-VPJ. (Gerry Manning)

Another view of PP-VQK, looking smart in Varig's newer colour scheme. (Gerry Manning)

PP-VMA, despite being the earliest of the Varig DC-10s, carried the new colour scheme for a number of years before being sold in 1999. (Bob O'Brien Collection)

Hong Kong's Kai Tak airport forms a familiar backdrop for the arrival for MD-11 PP-VPK. (Bob O'Brien Collection)

PP-VQJ in an updated version of the Varig scheme. (Richard Vandervord)

Varig was proud of its Star Alliance membership and was happy to paint PP-VTH with its logo. (Richard Vandervord)

Varig celebrated 50 years as an airline in 1977 and painted several aircraft in a special scheme, such as this carried by PP-VOK, a Boeing 767-300ER. (Gerry Manning)

Another example of the Boeing 767-300ER series, PP-VOI. (Gerry Manning)

PP-VNR was a Boeing 767-200ER that left the Varig fleet in 2004. (Gerry Manning)

This -300 series, PP-VOK, also wore the '50 Years' colours for a while. (Gerry Manning)

The basic scheme on PR-VAB is explained by the fact that it was leased for less than a year. (Bob O'Brien Collection)

Despite being one of the few Airbus widebodies in the fleet, PP-VND stayed with the airline for nine years. (Bob O'Brien Collection)

PP-VNS, a Boeing 767-200, was with Varig for about 16 years. (Gerry Manning)

Another long-service aircraft with Varig was PP-VNR. (Michael Prophet)

The basic colour scheme on series -300 PP-VTC reflects the fact that it was leased from Euro Atlantic Airways. (Richard Vandervord)

The same basic scheme was applied to PR-VAB, which was leased for less than a year. (Richard Vandervord)

Series -200ER PP-VNP was eventually converted to a freighter. (Richard Vandervord)

A selection of the Star Alliance logos adorns this Boeing 767-200ER. (Richard Vandervord)

PP-VOB, a 747-300, was delivered to Varig in June 1988. (Richard Vandervord)

Following its service with Varig, PP-VNH, a 747-300, was converted into a freighter. (Richard Vandervord)

This example, PP-VNI, was also converted into a freighter for Atlas Air. (Gerry Manning)

PP-VOA was delivered to Varig in April 1988 and stayed with the airline for 12 years. (Gerry Manning)

The scene is Frankfurt, and PP-VNB is being towed to another parking area. (Gerry Manning)

PP-VNH again, but this time wearing the original Varig scheme. (Richard Vandervord)

PP-VOC taxies onto stand at Amsterdam's Schiphol Airport. (Michael Prophet)

Chapter 5

The Widebodies Arrive, 1980–2000

Even though Varig operated a very mixed fleet, caused to some degree by its takeover of other airlines, the results when it came to ordering new aircraft its evaluation processes were long and painstaking. When the time came to decide between the Boeing 747 and the DC-10, Varig took two years over its decision and eventually came down on the side of the DC-10, a decision driven to some extent by the 1973 oil crisis, which had brought about a significant increase in fuel costs. As a result, three of the larger version, the DC-10-30, were ordered. Varig had ordered the type to service the routes that did not provide enough passengers to make economical use of the 747s. The first aircraft arrived on 29 May 1974 and was the first widebody aircraft to arrive in Latin America. The first Rio–New York flight with the tri-jet took place on 1 July 1974. The second was delivered on 18 June. They were registered as PP-VMA and VMB, and soon put into service, with one aircraft performing the route to Europe, Rio–Lisbon–Frankfurt–Copenhagen for the first time on 24 June, followed by the Rio–New York service on 1 July. Other destinations that were later served included London, Milan, Oporto and Zurich. These were followed by additional new destinations such as Panama, Cape Town and Bogotá. By the standards of the day, the DC-10 offered sophisticated technology, particularly regarding powerplants, flight control systems and cabin interiors. These were configured in typical uncramped Varig style, with a standard layout being 12 first class, 36 business and 181 economy seats. To mark the launch of the new type, new cabin crew uniforms and a bright orange and yellow interior were introduced.

The Cruzado Plan

The cruzado was the unit of currency in Brazil during the 1980s. In 1986, the government introduced measures designed to tackle Brazil's ever-present inflation, which had plagued the Brazilian economy for so many years. The measures outlined in the plan included a general price freeze and a freeze on the exchange rate for foreign currencies. Overall, the plan failed, but along the way, it had a severe effect on Varig's finances. Air fares had been included in the price freeze, and, whilst the freeze on the exchange rate helped to some extent with the airline's foreign currency expenses, the plan began to unravel over the succeeding months, and before long inflation had begun to rise again. The public debt became enormous, and by the end of 1986, inflation was in triple digits. The effect on Varig's revenue can be imagined.

The introduction into the Varig fleet of an Airbus in 1981 was a marked change from what previously had been an almost all-Boeing fleet. Despite being a widebody, the A300-B4 had a limited range and was suitable only for short- and medium-haul operations. Varig placed it on its denser domestic services, such as the routes along the eastern coast of Brazil, but it also operated into Miami with intermediate stops. Just two aircraft were ordered, with the second aircraft being received from Airbus on 23 June 1982. Varig had become the majority shareholder in its erstwhile competitor Cruzeiro do Sul in 1975, though both carriers continued to operate under separate titles. Cruzeiro had also ordered two

Embraer ERJ-145EP PT-SPL is towed across the apron at Santos Dumont. (Bob O'Brien Collection)

A300s and these were later absorbed into the Varig fleet. The aircraft was known as 'the silent giant', since it was significantly quieter than the narrowbody jets in service at the time. Many of Brazil's larger airports are close to urban areas and, as long ago as the late 1970s, there were night-flying restrictions in place at these airports. Cruzeiro received their two aircraft on 20 and 26 June 1980. The first flight took place on 1 July between São Paulo and Buenos Aires, followed soon afterwards by the east coast route northwards to Miami. However, the US authorities did not like the idea of an aircraft painted in Cruzeiro's colours operating on a route for which Varig had the licence, since they were, in effect, two different companies, and asked that, in future, only aircraft with the Varig titles be allowed to operate on the route.

The first aircraft in Varig colours, PP-VND, arrived on 3 July 1981, with the second being registered PP-VNE. The first route to be operated was between São Paulo and Chile's capital, Santiago. As other widebodies began to join the fleet, the A300s became restricted to domestic flights and one major international service to Buenos Aires. One advantage of the A300 was that it was able to use the downtown airport at Congonhas. However, with the opening of the new airport at Guarulhos in January 1985, international scheduled traffic was moved there, and this advantage was lost. As with the CV 990, the operation of just four aircraft of a totally different type put a considerable economic strain on the carrier's operations and, in December 1989, PP-VNE was sold to Japan Air System with PP-VND going to Air Jamaica in June 1990. Of the two Cruzeiro aircraft, PP-CLA also went to Air Jamaica, with the second aircraft, PP-CLB, following its stablemate to Japan.

On 1 September 1982, Varig followed a number of other carriers by introducing an executive class. A DC-10 on the Rio–Miami route was chosen for this purpose. As with other airlines, the status of executive class lay somewhere between first and economy, offering more spacious seating and a higher standard of service. Nevertheless, economy seats were still extremely popular, with lower fares and simpler service levels. With one eye on the competition, Varig had no option but to keep the economy fares as low as possible. The number of first class seats was gradually reduced to 12, allowing business class to be configured with a minimum of 38 seats, but at the very front of the aircraft, the service and comfort was second to none. At mealtimes on long-haul flights, drinks would arrive, followed by hot

Following Varig's problems, this aircraft was transferred to the Brazilian Air Force in 2005. (Bob O'Brien Collection)

and cold canapés, Beluga caviar, Strasbourg Foie Gras, melon with Parma ham and onion soup. Salads, main course, including a full gaucho barbecue, followed, and finally dessert and French cheeses were offered.

By this time, carriers in other parts of the world with long-haul routes were looking seriously at the Boeing 747, which had made its first flight in January 1970 with Pan Am. Varig saw that the 747 would now fit nicely into its route network, able to carry the ever-increasing number of passengers. The first two aircraft, series -200s, offering a larger upper deck and more power than the -100 series, arrived in Brazil in 1981. PP-VNA arrived in January, having originally been sold to and painted in the colours of Libyan Arab Airlines, an order which had not been taken up. PP-VNB, with a similar background, arrived in February of the same year. Both aircraft were soon operating on the Rio–New York route. The third aircraft of the batch, PP-VNC, arrived in March 1981. A fourth aircraft arrived from South African Airways in April 1987 and operated until August 1988. During this time, it carried the registration PP-VNW. They now began to be used on the routes from Rio de Janeiro to Paris and Frankfurt. These three aircraft represented the -200 series operated by the carrier, but as a larger version, the -300, became available, Varig ordered five of this series. The first aircraft, PP-VNH, was delivered as a combi aircraft, fitted with a rear cargo door. The remaining four -300s were acquired as standard passenger aircraft. Of these, PP-VNI was delivered in December 1985, with PP-VOA, VOB and VOC following between April and May 1988.

In April 1990, Rubel Thomas was elected as president of Ruben Berta Foundation (RBF), with a view to steer the airline through what was clearly a difficult period. Several new domestic and international routes were added. The São Paulo–Johannesburg–Bangkok–Hong Kong route began in 1993, followed by additional cities in the US, such as Orlando, Washington DC, Atlanta, and Chicago. The older Boeing 747s and McDonnell DC-10s were now being replaced by the newer versions of 747s and MD-11s, which had joined the fleet in 1991. These were used to serve New York, Paris and Rome, and the newly opened route to Hong Kong. However, the US market, which had been divided between Pan

This FH-227B joined the fleet following the Paraense, but it was seen as an interim aircraft, so the full titles were not applied. (Stefano Pagiola)

Am and Varig, changed radically. In 1992, Pan Am went bankrupt and was replaced on routes to Brazil by American Airlines, joined by TransBrasil, VASP, United Airlines, Continental Airlines and Delta Air Lines. As a result, ticket prices and load factors decreased. In order to reduce its debts, Varig decided to sell some of its aircraft to investors and banks, then lease them back, in order to keep maintain the operation.

In 1991, as part of a major restructuring, Varig had to cut more than 2,500 jobs and close ticket offices. Although the domestic routes were profitable, the carrier was losing money on international passenger operations. Rubel Thomas was replaced by Carlos Engels in April 1995, but his tenure was short-lived, when, unusually, the RBF intervened in the management decision-making process of what, by now, was becoming a financially troubled airline. He was replaced by Fernando Pinto, the former president of Rio-Sul and the son of a Varig pilot, who had led Rio-Sul through unprecedented growth. At the time, Varig was US$2.5bn in debt, about half of which was costs owed to leasing companies.

In an attempt to maintain customer loyalty, Varig launched a loyalty rewards programme called 'Smiles' in 1994, which soon became the biggest of its type in Latin America. A year later, the company acquired a 49 per cent stake in the Uruguayan flag carrier Pluna, and Rio-Sul purchased the domestic carrier Nordeste.

With the 747 now firmly established as the long-haul aircraft of choice for Varig, the introduction of the -400 brought Boeing further orders from the carrier. Two aircraft were ordered initially, registered PP-VPG and VPH. These were preceded by a lease aircraft carrying registration PP-VPI. This aircraft had originally been placed by Canadian Airlines International, but the order was not taken up and it was delivered in May 1991. The remaining two aircraft were delivered from Boeing in June 1992 and April 1993 and were initially put to work on the Sao Paulo–Rome service, later serving on the routes to Frankfurt, Buenos Aires and Nagoya, in Japan. Varig also used the larger version on its new route to Bangkok and Hong Kong, via Johannesburg. The financial problems of Varig were not helped by paying

The Boeing 777-200ER was the last widebody to be operated by Varig. This example, PP-VRA, was only in service for five years before it was repossessed in 2006. (Richard Vandervord)

the enormous leasing costs of such large and expensive aircraft, and Varig found these costs, together with the ever-present Brazilian inflation, to be too great for its economical operation. As a result, all three aircraft were returned to the lessor in late 1994 and were transferred to Air New Zealand. As the newer versions of the 747 were arriving, the series -200s were taken out of service and converted to freighters for Air Hong Kong.

As part of the fleet renovation process, Varig carried out a study on the Boeing 767. The version that most appealed to it carried the -ER (Extended Range) suffix, indicating that the range of this series was significantly greater at 6,590 miles (12,100km) than the 3,900 miles (7,200km) offered on the standard -200 model. It believed that on some of the thinner long-haul routes, such an aircraft would fulfil its requirements. The ER series were equipped with more fuel-efficient General Electric CF6 engines, which also enabled sophisticated flight management systems to be fitted. Varig placed an order directly with Boeing but, in the meantime, leased two aircraft from other operators.

In June 1986, a version was leased from Transportes Aéreos de Centroamericano (TACA) and registered as PP-VNL, followed by PP-VNM from Braathens SAFE Air Transport of Norway in September 1986. Both these aircraft were the earlier versions and thus fitted with the Pratt & Whitney JT9D engines. An order for new aircraft had been placed and, on 2 July 1987, the first of the -200 series, a standard version, PP-VNN, was received. All of these aircraft were fitted with the CF6 engine. The remaining five aircraft had all been delivered by the end of August 1987. These were registered in the block PP-VNO to VNS. They were used on routes within Latin America, and occasional charters, sometimes as far as Lisbon. However, the aircraft did not stay long in Varig colours, and, by March 2003, all been returned to the lessor, GE Capital Aviation Services (GECAS). Only PP-VNO, also a standard version, remained in the fleet, for possible use on charter flights, but it too was returned just a month later. Varig had just eight of the type.

Varig now turned its attention to the extended version: the -300ER. The fuselage of the -200 had been extended by the use of two 'plugs' inserted before and after the wings. Both plugs were 21ft (6.43m) in length. A choice of engines was available, with the Pratt & Whitney 4000, the General Electric

The same aircraft in the standard Varig scheme. Varig operated eight Boeing 777s with a mixture of GE 90 and PW 4007 engines. (Richard Vandervord)

CF6 and the Rolls-Royce RB211 as options. All of these were more fuel efficient, state-of-the-art high by-pass turbofan engines. The higher weight of the -300 meant that the range was slightly reduced, but still a very satisfactory 5,980 miles (11,070km). Varig chose the CF6 for the aircraft delivered directly from Boeing, since these had previously been fitted to the -200ERs. The first aircraft was delivered in December 1989, followed by three further aircraft in February, June and August 1990. All four were allocated registrations in the block PP-VOI to VOL, with PP-VOI being painted in a Star Alliance colour scheme. They were put into service on the longer routes where passenger loads were thinner, for example to the US and Europe, and the major cities of the Brazilian northeast, such as Recife and Fortaleza, together with other major cities within Latin America. They were also used periodically for charter flights. In December 2004, PP-VOL was returned to the leasing company, followed by PP-VOK, which had carried the 50 years celebration colours. in May 2005 and PP-VPW in June 2005.

Two additional aircraft were acquired from Canadian Airlines in 1997, and registered PP-VPV and VPW, with two others joining the fleet from Euro Atlantic Airways in 2003. These were registered PP-VTC and VTE but differed from the other aircraft in that they were fitted with the Pratt & Whitney 4060 powerplants. Both aircraft had left the fleet by mid-2009. The five remaining -300s were still part of the fleet until Varig's demise in 2006. PP-VOI and VOJ went to Business Air in Thailand in June and April 2010, respectively, with PP-VPV going to Euro Atlantic Airways in December 2006 and VTC following in June 2009. PP-VTE left the fleet only in 2008.

Varig acquired a further six DC-10-30s, the first of which was delivered on 31 July 1980. Their registrations were allocated in the block PP-VMT to PP-VMY. The final aircraft in the batch was delivered in June 1981. The earlier aircraft, PP-VMB and PP-VMD, were sold in 1998, and in order to reduce the number of aircraft on its books, Varig sold and leased back PP-VMA in September 1998, but it left the fleet the following year. Both PP-VMX and VMY were leased to Garuda Indonesia for several months during 1994, before being sold to Northwest Airlines in the US in 1999. Also during 1994, Brazil won the World Cup football final in California and PP-VMD was painted in special scheme to bring the victorious team back to Rio from Los Angeles.

Of the remaining aircraft, PP-VMO and VMP had been leased and were returned to CP Air after a year. PP-VMQ left the fleet in 1999 to go to Pluna in Uruguay. PP-VMR was ex-Singapore Airlines and remained in the fleet for just a year. PP-VMS and PP-VMZ stayed in the fleet for 12 years before being sold back to McDonnell Douglas. During the late 1980s, Varig had begun to operate a cargo version of the DC-10, under VarigLog, designated the DC-10-30F. These were PP-VMT and VMU.

Based on their experience with the DC-10s, it seemed logical for Varig to order its successor, the MD-11. This more modern version was able to offer considerable advantages over the DC-10, not least of which was the fitting of winglets, which it was claimed would reduce fuel usage significantly. Computerised systems had been fitted throughout the aircraft, including the so-called glass cockpit. The first two aircraft arrived on 12 November 1991, with Varig once again being the first airline in Latin America to operate the type. These were initially put into operation flying Sao Paulo–Rio–Paris–Amsterdam, and later other long-haul flights, and were registered PP-VOP and -VOQ. When required, due to high seasonal loads, they would also be deployed on major routes within South America and occasionally even domestic routes. Two further aircraft, PP-VPJ and VPK, arrived in December 1992, with the final aircraft of a batch of six arriving a year later. These were registered as PP-VPL and VPM.

With new and existing routes firmly established, Varig needed more MD-11s, but by now the carrier was beset by economic problems and unable to make deals for new aircraft. It so happened that Garuda Indonesia was looking to offload its MD-11s, and Varig was keen to take them. PP-VPN was the first to arrive in December 1996, followed by two further aircraft in April and December 1997. These were PP-VPO and VPP. In 1998, two further aircraft arrived from Garuda. These became PP-VQH and PP-VQI. This last aircraft was designated -ER, one of only five built, meaning that the aircraft had been fitted with an additional fuel tank in the forward cargo hold, thus enabling the aircraft to travel an additional 400 miles (740km) in comparison with the standard version. Three of these were originally delivered to Garuda and Varig took them over. PP-VQI was delivered in September 1998, VQJ was received in October 1999 and finally VQK in November 1999. In addition to the European routes, the aircraft were used for services to Johannesburg, Bangkok and Hong Kong. By 2000, the MD-11s were also being used on services to Copenhagen, Los Angeles, Miami, Tokyo and Nagoya.

By this time, almost all the Boeing 747s and DC-10s had been removed from service and replacements were required. In 2000, Varig had taken two MD-11s from VASP, its major competitor. These became PP-VQL and VQM, both of which were delivered in May 2000 and used to replace PP-VOP and VOQ. A further ex-VASP aircraft arrived in June 2001 and became PP-VQX, thus releasing PP-VPL and VPM.

Ongoing financial difficulties within the airline meant that the acquisition of new aircraft was out of the question, but when Varig next entered the marketplace to augment the fleet of MD-11s, its options were more limited. It turned to Swissair for further aircraft, but there was a problem. The MD-11s in Varig's current fleet were all fitted with General Electric CF6 engines, whereas Swissair's MD-11s were fitted with Pratt & Whitney 4462 engines, which meant that additional spares, training, and tooling would be required for their operation. In 2003, three of the former Swissair aircraft joined the fleet, followed by a further five in 2004. These were registered in the blocks PP-VTF to VTH and PP-VTI to VTK, then PP-VTP and VTU, making eight aircraft in total.

In 2005, eight of the MD-11s were returned to the lessors. These were PP-VPJ, VPK, VPL, VPM, VQM, VTF, VPN and VPP. Several of these aircraft were later converted to freighters. All-cargo versions of the MD-11 were becoming increasingly common and, in 2005, VarigLog began to operate two MD-11Fs, PR-LGD and LGE. These were originally operated by Korean Air, and, following service with them, both aircraft had been fitted with large cargo doors.

During this time, many changes had taken place in aviation, the greatest of which was deregulation in both the US and Europe. This was also implemented in Brazil and, in 1990, the Brazilian commercial aviation system was deregulated. This meant that airlines were now free to fly wherever they wanted and charge the most appropriate fares, instead of asking for permission from the authorities that had previously governed both route networks and fares. This model had worked in the US, though some airlines that had been unable to adapt to the new standards did not survive. Overall, consumers were pleased that ticket prices were now much lower and that there was now much greater competition. One effect of deregulation on Brazil can be explained as follows: before deregulation, only Varig and Pan Am had operated flights between the US and Brazil. In 1992, Pan Am went bankrupt and, in less than a year, six other carriers were operating on the route. These were American Airlines, Continental, Delta, United, TransBrasil and VASP. In previous years, the two major carriers had regularly flown with full loads paying high fares, even in economy. Now those flights were half empty and ticket prices were significantly lower.

It was not just on the international routes that Varig was suffering. The appearance of TAM (Táxi Aéreo Marília), a rapidly expanding domestic airline based in São Paulo, had meant that Varig's principal domestic routes were now facing intense competition. The Varig subsidiary, Rio-Sul, was operating with F-27s on many routes, but TAM was already introducing the Fokker 100. As TAM continued to grow in the 1990s, Varig ordered Embraer ERJ-145s and Boeing 737-500s, fitting both aircraft out with reduced seating capacity in order to compete, at least in terms of comfort, with TAM. TAM responded by raising the stakes further, going into the market for Airbus A319s and A320s and also upgrading its passenger service both on the ground and in the air. In 1998, TAM entered the international market with flights to Miami and Paris, using an A330-200 with a cabin fitted to a high specification, having individual monitors on the seat backs in all classes and seats that reclined flat in business class. This contrasted sharply with the earlier versions of Varig's MD-11s, which were beginning to look rather tired.

Whilst the long-haul routes were being developed, Varig had not lost sight of its domestic operation and had to consider what would replace the older Boeing 737-200s. The choice was the Boeing 737-700NG, which was similar in size to the -300 but incorporated many of the newer advances in technology. A new cabin design meant small monitor screens for the passengers, additional luggage space and a re-designed cabin. The flight deck layout had been adapted so that it was similar to its much larger cousin, the Boeing 777. The more modern CFM56-7 engines, although slightly larger than their predecessors, were quieter and more economical. As with the earlier version, the aircraft were used on the domestic services, including the Air Bridge, together with the shorter-haul international routes within South America, such as Asunción and Montevideo.

New logo, new fleet

In 1996, Varig, having maintained the same corporate logo since the mid-1950s, decided on a radical change. This was done to celebrate its 70th anniversary, and management had decided on a complete change of image. Gone were the familiar blue pinstripes and the depiction of Icarus known all around the world. After the difficult times the airline had faced, it was considered that a new image was required to reflect this. The compass rose, also recognised as a star, was modernised and its colour was changed to gold. The circle surrounding it was dropped. The title 'Brasil' – the Portuguese spelling for Brazil - was written in calligraphic style, which if viewed in a certain way could be seen as either a 'z' or an 's'. The tail and belly of the aircraft were painted in dark blue. As part of its celebrations, Varig took the opportunity to join the Star Alliance airline rewards group in May 1997, which at the time included Lufthansa, United Airlines, Scandinavian Airlines and Air Canada. Ansett Australia and Air New

Zealand also joined the alliance during that year. This gave the group a network of 720 destinations in 110 countries, operating a combined fleet of 1,650 aircraft.

Varig placed its largest ever order for new aircraft the following year. A total of 24 aircraft were ordered, with 15 further aircraft on option. Included in the deal were Boeing 767-300ER, 737-700, 737-800 and 777-200 models. Varig was to become the first airline in Latin America to operate the Boeing 737-700. The plan was for the Boeing 737-700s to replace the early model Boeing 727s and Airbus A300. The first of these, a Boeing 737-700, was received in November 1998, and registered as PP-VQA. Three further aircraft arrived a month later and were registered in the block PP-VQB to VQD. A fourth aircraft, PP-VQE, was received in January 1999.

The early MD-11s were retired from the fleet in 1998, the same year in which TAM inaugurated flights from Brazil to Miami with the Airbus A330. The Varig MD-11 was unable to compete – a situation that would last until November 2001, when Varig received its first Boeing 777-200 for routes to the US and Europe. Its Boeing 727s and Airbus A300s were retired in 1998. Owing to competition from other carriers, the international network was redesigned, dropping unprofitable routes to destinations in Africa, Canada, Ecuador, Costa Rica and the Caribbean. On 2 June 1999, the last Boeing 747 left the fleet.

Behind the scenes though, dark clouds were beginning to gather over Varig and thoughts of additional purchases had to be curtailed. In fact, it became clear that Varig was struggling to make the lease payments on its existing aircraft. In 2003, all the 737-700s were returned, but in June of that year, Varig completed a full merger with two of its subsidiaries, Nordeste and Rio-Sul. Nordeste was a regional carrier based in Salvador, the capital of Bahia state, in the northeast of Brazil, and operated a network throughout that area. Rio-Sul, although based in Rio, had a similar operation in the southeast of Brazil. As a result of this, two 737-700s that had been part of Rio-Sul's fleet reappeared in Varig's colours in September 2002, but carrying the same registrations, PR-SAF and PR-SAG.

The first two of four 747-200 combis began service with Varig in March 1981. Three, including PP-VNA-C, were ordered new from Boeing and were fitted with General Electric CF6 engines. The fourth was Pratt & Whitney-powered and bought from South African Airways in 1987. Other 747s that joined the fleet were standard passenger versions.

To understand Varig's situation from the beginning, it is necessary to go back to the mid-1960s and some high-level domestic politics. At the time, the military regime had just come into power and Panair do Brasil was the *de facto* flag carrier. The major shareholder in Panair, Mario Wallace Simonsen, was a good friend of Juscelino Kubitschek, who had been the president of Brazil between 1956 and 1961. During his tenure, he was responsible for the re-siting of the capital from Rio de Janeiro to Brasilia. In a coup d'état, the military government took control of the country during 31 March–1 April 1964. João Goulart, the president who was deposed, was also a friend of both, thus the military were not disposed to dealing kindly with them. On 10 February 1965, Panair do Brasil's president received a telegram informing him that the company's operations had been suspended. Five days later, the company was declared bankrupt, and it was announced that the domestic routes would be transferred to Cruzeiro do Sul and the international routes to Varig. As previously mentioned, Varig was able to undertake Panair's international routes immediately, so there was no loss of service. From this, it is clear that the demise of Panair do Brasil had been planned for some time before this event.

It became apparent from this episode that the government of the day was determined to have a significant say in the operation of any Brazilian airline, and therefore the airlines would have to maintain good relationships with it. Without this, any attempt to buy new aircraft and open new routes would be difficult, if not impossible. This was easier for Varig, as the *de facto* flag carrier, but not so much for its competitors, VASP and TransBrasil, although they continued to operate normally. This situation had continued until 1985, when a democratic government was restored to power.

Chapter 6

The Decline and Fall, 2000–06

Following the merger with Rio-Sul in 2002, another Boeing 737 variant entered the Varig fleet. This time it was the Boeing 737-500, the smallest version of the more recent series to be built. It had been designed to carry up to 130 passengers in a single-class cabin, and it had fitted well into Rio-Sul's route structure. In Rio-Sul's configuration, it had been operated with just 108 seats, a spacious layout for short-haul domestic operation. In Varig service, they were used on the thinner routes. Nordeste had operated four similar aircraft, all sourced from the used market. This meant that Varig was now operating a total of 20 aircraft, 16 from Rio-Sul and four from Nordeste. Of the Nordeste aircraft, two had been received in October 1997 and a further two in October 1999 and March 2001. The type was used to replace the Embraer 120 and the Fokker 50s, which had been operating on both carriers' routes, and with the introduction of jets came an increase in passenger demand. Some of the 737-300s began to be switched to these routes and, in 2001, the -700 series was also introduced. To cope with demand and increase profitability, the -500s were reconfigured with 120 seats. There was a long-term plan to replace the -500 with larger versions in order to standardise the fleet, but this never came to fruition.

In 2000, Varig came under the administration of Ozires Silva, a doyen of Brazilian aviation, having been the lead engineer of the Embraer Bandeirante project and, ultimately, the president of the company. Although he only stayed at Varig for two and a half years, he began with a major restructuring of the company, with the aim of making the RBF more powerful and reducing the powers of the president-director. Also, on 28 January 2000, all-cargo operations were united under a new airline named VarigLog. VarigLog, the former cargo arm of Varig, ultimately bought Varig for US$24m, but in doing so assumed its huge debts. The creditors did not want VarigLog to buy the airline, because from their perspective they would be better off if the airline was declared fully bankrupt, but the decision of the bankruptcy judge overruled their wishes and so the airline was sold. VarigLog wanted Varig to cancel most flights and start again, but the regulator would not allow this. Despite the reforms, Varig had posted a deficit for first time in its history: US$81m by the end of 2000, and then US$285m in the following year.

VarigLog

On 25 August 2000, in order to cater for the increasing demand for air freight Varig, which had operated both combi and pure cargo aircraft for many years, set up a subsidiary called VarigLog, a shortened form of Varig Logistica. The carrier was based at Jardim Aeroporto in Campo Belo near São Paulo and began operations as a separate entity in September 2000. It soon became the largest cargo carrier in Latin America. Initially, a total of nine of Varig's Boeing 727s were converted for this purpose, with four of these being sourced from the used aircraft market. One of these, PP-VLD, which had been delivered new from Boeing in 1970, was later bought at auction by former Varig employees on 23 October 2020, with the intention of putting it on display in Porto Alegre.

The fleet initially comprised five Boeing 727-100Fs, four Boeing 727-200Fs and three McDonnell Douglas DC-10-30Fs. As the 'F' suffix suggests, all had been converted to freighters, and most had originally been retired from Varig's main fleet. Two MD-11s, also converted for cargo carrying, were added to the fleet during March and June of 2007, thus making it the first airline in Latin America to operate an all-cargo version of the type. These were PR-LGD and PR-LGE. Later, two Boeing 737-400Fs (in 2010 and 2011, respectively) and Boeing 757-200PCFs were initially added to the fleet. All of these were leased, and the total number operated was seven, all but one of which began operating in 2007. All the aircraft were returned to the lessors when VarigLog was declared bankrupt.

The carrier continued to operate as such until it was bought by a consortium known as Volo do Brasil in December 2005, as part of the break-up of Varig's assets. The strict laws regarding foreign capital involvement in Brazilian industry meant that the negotiations were not concluded until June 2006. Volo, which was controlled by the US hedge fund MatlinPatterson, needed additional authorisation from Brazil's Civil Aviation Authority before the acquisition could become effective. However, many observers believe the approval of VarigLog's acquisition in 2005 alone should have resolved the foreign ownership question.

After two unsuccessful attempts to auction the airline as a complete entity, the bankruptcy court took the decision to split the airline in two different judicial entities, to be informally known as 'Old Varig' and 'New Varig.' Following the completion of these negotiations, Volo bought the parent company, the so-called 'New Varig' in July 2006, but this situation lasted only a year. 'New Varig' was then stripped from the Volo group when, on 28 March 2007, Gol Linhas Aéreas, the Brazilian low-cost carrier, formally acquired 'New Varig' for US$320m. Between June 2007 and June 2009, VarigLog operated under an agreement with the Brazilian arm of FedEx.

Despite its promising beginnings, VarigLog quickly began to accumulate debts, and on 3 March 2009 was placed under bankruptcy protection. The company then came under the ownership of Synergy Group, a conglomerate based in São Paulo, which also owned Avianca, the Colombian flag-carrier, and TACA Airlines, based in El Salvador. However, Synergy's participation did little to bolster the VarigLog's fortunes, and it was finally declared bankrupt on 27 September 2012.

In 2001, Varig had received its first Boeing 777-200ERs, as well as Boeing 737-800s. The two types became the backbone of the fleet, with the 777 replacing the MD-11 and the 737-800 replacing the Boeing 737-200, plus most of the 737-300s. The -800 series were fitted with winglets, an innovation designed to improve overall performance, whilst at the same time reducing fuel consumption. Two of the new series arrived in September and October 2001, respectively, and were registered PP-VSA and VSB. The aircraft operated on some domestic routes, but also to Buenos Aires, Lima and Santiago. When the initial order was placed, the plan was to order 10 of them, with options for up to 32, but by this time, Varig's financial situation was such that only the first two aircraft were received. They remained in the fleet until the end of operations in 2006.

The final derivative of the 737 that Varig operated was the -400. This was a stretched version of the -300, which in Varig's configuration, was typically configured with 142 seats: 12 business and 130 economy or 156 seats in an all-economy cabin. The first four of these, previously owned by TransBrasil, were added to the fleet in June 2000. Three were re-registered as PP-VQQ to VQS. The fourth aircraft retained its TransBrasil registration as PP-TEO. Additionally, to cover the stalled deal for the -800s, PP-VTL was acquired from Futura International Airlines of Spain, PP-VTM arrived in May 2004, followed by in June by PP-VTN and VTO. These had been previously owned by Asiana of South Korea. All four aircraft remained in the fleet until 2006.

The Boeing 777 was one of the last new aircraft types to join the Varig fleet. Generally considered as a replacement for both the Boeing 747 and the MD-11 and a competitor for the Airbus A330, the 777 had sold very successfully around the world. Varig had selected it as an MD-11 replacement. Its budgetary crisis was still in evidence, and as a result of this, only two aircraft were received directly from Boeing. The first aircraft, PP-VRA, a series -200, arrived on 3 November 2001, and ten days later made a familiarisation flight from Rio to Porto Alegre. The aircraft was used on the Rio–Sao Paulo–London–Copenhagen route. The second aircraft, PP-VRB, arrived on 19 November 2001, and its first flight was on the Rio–São Paulo–Paris–Amsterdam route. In an unusual move, connected to the airline's 75th anniversary, Varig named both aircraft. *Otto Meyer*, Varig's founder was applied to PP-VRA, while *Ruben Berta*, the first employee of Varig, was applied to PP-VRB, with both aircraft carrying a large '75' in the area of the forward door.

Between 2003 and 2004, it was clear that Varig were running into serious financial difficulties. In order to deal with this, the airline set up a full restructuring programme, which included merging with Rio-Sul and Nordeste. The merger resulted in Varig having a fleet of more than 120 aircraft, including the Boeing 737-500s and Embraer 145s that had previously been owned by these carriers. During 2004, Varig had also received Boeing 757-200s, which seemed to fit well into their route structure. These had been brought into the fleet to cover medium-haul routes within South America. All four aircraft arrived during 2004, with two aircraft, PP-VTQ and VTR, arriving in August, followed by PP-VTS in September and the final aircraft, PP-VTT, in December. All of them had previously been operated by Iberia. The routes chosen were to Caracas, Aruba in the Netherlands Antilles, Buenos Aires and Lima. Further services were operated to Asunción and long-haul domestic destinations. The aircraft spent a relatively short time with Varig, as they were returned to the lessor by the end of 2006. Apparently undaunted by these problems, Varig continued to expand its route system, having signed a codeshare agreement with Air China to operate the São Paulo–Munich–Beijing route.

In 2004, two further Boeing 777-200 series were received. On February 27, PP-VRC, formerly with both British Airways and Air Algerie, arrived. This aircraft was already nine years old. PP-VRD had a similar history and had actually been delivered a month earlier on 27 January. However, its tenure in Varig service was relatively short, and it was returned to the lessor in November 2006 and was actually the first ever Boeing 777 to be scrapped in January 2007. It was just 11 years old. Two further aircraft were delivered; these were the ER versions. PP-VRE and VRF came from United Airlines and had been fitted with the PW4090 engines. The previous four aircraft, which were not the ER version, had been fitted with the standard GE90 engine, so once again Varig was faced with having to deal with two different types of engine on the same airframe. Not only that, but having leased the aircraft from different companies, the aircraft were non-standard. For example, the ER versions were configured with 22 seats in first class and 70 in business class, which was totally incompatible with the Brazilian market. Varig would have reconfigured the cabin in normal circumstances, but by now the resources were not available. PP-VRI joined the fleet in February 2005 and PP-VRJ arrived in April 2005. Again, these were ex-United aircraft and not the ER version. PP-VRH had been reserved but was not taken up.

PP-VRB, VRD and VRF were taken out of service in April 2006 and PP-VRE was impounded at JFK Airport in New York and was already engineless by June 2006. PP-VRI was taken out of service after making the last flight on the route Manaus–Brasilia–Rio de Janeiro. PP-VRA was impounded in Rio de Janeiro after returning from Munich. The last two aircraft to remain flying were PP-VRC and VRJ, which were finally retired in July 2006. The combination of aircraft acquired from a number of different sources, and the dire financial situation of Varig during this time meant that the Boeing 777 was never a very successful aircraft for the airline.

The beginning of the end

A newcomer to the scene, low-cost airline Gol Airlines, had begun operations in 2001, with VASP and TransBrasil having to cut fares in response. This had a serious effect on Varig too, the loss of passengers to competitors causing Varig to lose its top position in the domestic market share (in terms of passengers per kilometre), to TAM, for the first time since 1961. The 11 September attacks in 2001 affected airlines worldwide, and Varig was no exception, with the loss of revenue further weakening Varig's operational and financial situation.

As discussed, the RBF merged the administration of Varig and its subsidiary Rio-Sul (which included the brand Nordeste). The three brands continued to operate separately, although the two regional carriers were still able to provide useful feeder services to Varig. Discussions with the aim of merging Varig with TAM took place during 2004, but these were unsuccessful, and, as a result, Varig fell to third place in the Brazilian domestic market share, behind TAM and Gol. The RBF, by its constitution, was 80 per cent owned by its employees. The rules provided that any member of the foundation could become its president, despite their skill level. The mindset of the foundation was totally against making employees redundant, but Varig was in decline and could not realistically continue to maintain the same staff levels. As a comparison, whilst TAM at that time had more than 80 aircraft, whilst Varig had only 60, but Varig had twice as many employees.

The 9/11 terrorist attacks had resulted in a major crisis worldwide in the aviation sector. With low-cost carrier Gol now on the scene and VASP and TransBrasil cutting fares in order to respond to both the newcomer and the decline in passengers, TAM took the decision to cancel international flights and reduce domestic frequencies. However, Varig did not react to the increase in competition and subsequent decrease in revenue. It continued to fly its domestic and international routes at the same fare levels as previously, but now with almost empty aircraft, thus accumulating huge losses and debts; by 2002, Varig's losses exceeded US$2bn. Following pressure from the government and the bankruptcy court, and in order to minimise the effects of competition, Varig and TAM signed a codeshare agreement on domestic routes, but this agreement only lasted until the end of 2003.

It was clear that as a result of the intense competition on all its routes, the financial health of the airline was declining rapidly. The first step was to restructure the company, and a close look was taken at the long-haul fleet. The Boeing 747s that had once produced so much revenue were now flying with many empty seats, yet they were only three years old. Such were Varig's leasing arrangements that even with a full load the aircraft could not pay for themselves. The three Boeing 747-400s had been returned in 1994. The constant depreciation of the Real, Brazil's national currency, against hard currencies, together with ever-present inflation meant that repayment of the loans on aircraft became increasingly difficult. In the case of the 747s, the loans had been provided by a Japanese bank, and the Yen had appreciated significantly against the Real during this time. Soon after this, Varig was forced to withdraw the remaining 747s, the 727-100s, the 737-300s and the DC-10s. It is fair to say that the 727-100s and 737-300s were reaching the end of their useful service lives anyway, but the problem was that Varig was now unable to negotiate credit with leasing companies with whom it needed to negotiate replacements.

The RBF was becoming increasingly concerned about the situation, and since it was set up to oversee the welfare of its staff members, it began to take a greater part in the day-to-day affairs of the airline. This was followed by a series of other dismissals between 2002 and 2006, when no less than nine different presidents were appointed. In 2001, with Gol entering the market, the airline business in Brazil had been turned on its head. Based in Rio de Janeiro and flagged as a low-cost carrier, it quickly became very popular and was now challenging not only Varig, but TAM, who until that time had been the leader in the domestic market.

The passengers soon realised that TAM's aircraft were newer and smarter than Varig's, though for a while the codeshare did improve Varig's load factors. Despite this, any possibility of closer cooperation, was ruled out by the RBF and Varig's employees, who firmly resisted all attempts to integrate the two carriers. The only possibility now was for a full merger between Varig and its subsidiaries, an idea put forward by the government, but the RBF did not agree with this idea either. An attempt by a company called NV Participações, which was 40 per cent owned by Varig personnel and 60 per cent by foreign investors, to take over the airline, was rejected in 2004. The Brazilian government then suggested a merger with Gol, but this was also rejected. Following this, a further attempt by the Brazilian government to solve the crisis involved a 20 per cent stake being offered from Euro Atlantic Airlines of Portugal, an airline normally specialising in dry leases and charters, together with a similar investment by LAN Airlines of Chile. This idea was put forward in December 2004, but was also unsuccessful, so the only answer was going to be the purchase of the company by a third party, or intervention by the government. Thus began the downfall of the airline.

As a result of the failure to find a buyer for Varig, the airline was forced to request the Commercial Bankruptcy and Reorganisation Court in Rio de Janeiro on 17 June 2005 for formal permission to reorganise the company. The request was granted on 22 June 2005. It also used the opportunity to request the US courts for protection from its creditors, principally the leasing companies to whom Varig owed significant amounts of money. In order to raise funds, the Court decided to sell two of Varig's subsidiaries. In November 2005, the maintenance centre, VEM Maintenance & Engineering, originally created in 2001, and ranked as one of the top ten in the world, was sold to a consortium owned by the Portuguese airline TAP. There were also rumours of a possible merger with TAP, but this never came to fruition.

As part of this process, the airline was divided into two portions, known informally as 'Old Varig' and 'New Varig.' 'Old Varig' then became judicially known as Viação Aérea Rio-Grandense. 'New Varig' became judicially known as VRG Linhas Aéreas. This was effectively a new airline formed with some assets of the original Varig, which had been auctioned on 14 July 2006. The legal procedures to enable this were finalised on 20 July 2006. The court ruling meant that from that day, VRG Linhas Aéreas and Viação Aérea Rio-Grandense were different legal entities and airlines.

From documents submitted to the court, it became apparent that 'Old Varig' had a balance sheet deficit of US$2.8bn, plus a further off-balance sheet debt of US$2bn. Flights were still being operated, but with a very reduced network; the international routes within South America were discontinued, together with those to Los Angeles and New York. The only solution for Varig was to sell its existing aircraft that were not subject to leasing arrangements to a bank or lessor and lease them back.

Following the court's decision, the so-called 'Old Varig' operated under a Recovery Order (similar to the Chapter 11 employed for such situations in the US). Two judges from the Business Court led the process. Once the bankruptcy protection had been lifted, it would have been possible for the airline to have continued to operate under the RBF, which at the time still owned 87 per cent of the Varig shares, but the RBF refused this option and allowed the judges to continue as judicial administrators of the company. During this time, in September 2006, 'Old Varig' sold its shares in Pluna, the Uruguayan flag carrier, in which it had a 49 per cent holding. The shares were bought by the Uruguayan government.

'Old Varig' suspended most of its operations, with the exception of the Rio–São Paulo Air Bridge, which remained in operation by means of a special agreement, in order not to disrupt the service. On 21 June 2006, exactly one month later after services were suspended, it was purchased at auction by Volo do Brasil, together with the parent company of VarigLog for US$128m excluding debts. A 10 per the redistribution process, thus escalating the entire process to a higher level in the Brazilian legal system. The Federal Appeals Court in Rio de Janeiro upheld ANAC's complaint, thus enabling ANAC to redistribute the assets. VRG then counter-appealed the ruling. On 26 September 2006, three judges, sitting in the Federal Appeals Court, overturned the award against ANAC, thus placing the situation back in square one.

In essence, the Federal Appeals Court had indeed ruled that route rights and slots were the property of the airline and not ANAC. As a result, ANAC cancelled the auction of Varig's unused route rights that had been scheduled for 16 October 2006.

Gol also took over part of 'Old Varig's' debt of an estimated US$45m. At that time, 'Old Varig' was still under bankruptcy protection. Gol had decided to allow the Varig brand to continue to operate, while Gol itself would continue to focus on its low-cost flights. The Gol transaction, via its subsidiary, Gol Transportes Inteligentes (GTI), required a US$98m cash payment, with the balance to be sourced through the allocation of non-voting shares to VarigLog and Volo, which had acquired 'New Varig' in June 2006. 'Old Varig' was not included in the deal, because it had been split off to Flex.

The flights that took place were restricted to scheduled and charter routes within South America and the Caribbean, using the 'Old Varig' Boeing 737-700s configured in two classes. Additionally, long-haul charters were operated to destinations in Africa, Europe and North America using the 767-300ERs in an all-economy configuration. These aircraft were also used on a wet-lease basis for a while; this is an arrangement whereby one operator provides another with a fully serviceable aircraft, a complete crew, maintenance, and insurance. The lessee pays by the hours operated. The scheme, however, did not last for more than a few months.

The VRG reservation system was gradually integrated into that of Gol's, but a few services continued to operate under Varig flight numbers until 20 August 2010. On this date, the Rio de Janeiro court finally declared 'Old Varig' and the two other companies in its group, Rio-Sul Linhas Aéreas and Nordeste Linhas Aéreas, bankrupt. In 2009, Gol began to repaint the 'Old Varig' aircraft that had been integrated into its fleet, a process which would last until 2014. For a while, some aircraft carried a hybrid scheme, although throughout this turbulent period the name Varig was no longer seen on its aircraft.

Gol committed to invest US$500m in VRG, including an immediate US$75m cash recapitalisation to be issued within 48 hours, and another US$75m investment within 30 days, the remainder be utilised to service its post-bankruptcy debts, but this solution was not well received by the union representing Varig's employees, who, on 31 July 2006, had obtained an injunction in a Rio de Janeiro labour court, which ordered the airline to use the US$75m cash injection to release unpaid salaries. For its part, Volo claimed that the monies were to be used for paying airport landing and handling fees and suppliers.

Volo had purchased the rights to use Varig's brand and that of its regional subsidiary, Rio-Sul, as well as the carrier's recently reduced fleet and route network. At that time, the carrier had only 13 operational aircraft serving a network of 25 domestic and international destinations. The new owner had declared that its immediate priorities would be a decrease in Varig's workforce, reducing it to less than 2,000 employees, down from the 10,000 who had been employed at the beginning of the year, but that it would increase the fleet to 25 aircraft. 'Old Varig' would retain an active air operator's certificate and would fly a single aircraft as Nordeste, the name of Varig's former regional subsidiary for northern Brazil. It was suggested that to pay off part of the debt, which was estimated at about US$3.2bn, the company would receive an annual royalty payment of at least US$20m for the next 20 years from 'New Varig'. The death of Varig was to prove slow and agonising.

The camaraderie that exists amongst airline employees at all levels is much greater than in many industries, and when an airline is forced to close down, the effect is like splitting up a family. During this dark period of the airline, many of the staff still turned up for work, even though they were not being paid. Some employees even brought items such as coffee from their own homes with which to serve the passengers.

A number of attempts were made by the RBF through the courts to keep 'Old Varig' alive, but the accumulated debts and the lack of routes and slots meant that their expectations were unrealistic. Many of the aircraft were flown into storage in Porto Alegre, while the leased aircraft were gradually returned to the lessors. The RBF had done their best to avoid the airline completely closing down, but inevitably the court ruling was the last act in this very sorry drama.

Addendum

Varig was, by no means, alone in becoming a major international airline to fail through bankruptcy. Pan Am and TWA in the US, Alitalia, Olympic, Sabena and Swissair in Europe, have all suffered the same fate. Some major international airlines survive today only because of government support. At its peak, Varig was a world-class airline, without a doubt comparable to those mentioned above. Some observers have blamed an inability to adapt to market conditions, others to domestic and sometimes international politics, and there is no doubt that all three situations played a major part in bringing down the airline. However, it must be said that operating such a mixed fleet, even under optimal conditions, puts an enormous strain on resources, both financial and human. The constant fluctuation in exchange rates and the imposition by successive governments of limits on air fares, despite increasing oil prices, and the requirement for Brazilians to have to deposit significant amounts of money before undertaking long-haul flights, significantly affected revenue, but were beyond the control of the carrier. Those parameters that the airline was in control of – management, staffing and some of the normal operating costs – were not always tightly controlled, and whilst the concept of a foundation in which the employees are major shareholders is good in theory, it too must be carefully controlled, to avoid abuse. It could be argued that, in some respects, the RBF was a contributory factor in Varig's downfall. The fact that it owned more than 80 per cent of the airline and that employees could not be dismissed, coupled with the considerable additional benefits that were available to members, such as free health care, put both ethical and financial constraints onto the carrier. Between 2002 and 2005, Varig had nine presidents, all of whom were dismissed by the foundation.

It must also be said that in the late 1960s and early 1970s, Varig's accident record left much to be desired, and this undoubtedly dissuaded potential passengers, both Brazilian and foreign, from flying with them. In the interests of balance though, it should be stated that flying was very different during those years. A perusal of the worldwide accident statistics for that decade makes very sobering reading. Many airfields in Brazil had little more than a landing strip and a hut, with no navigational aids. Even the more modern aircraft were equipped with what, by today's standards, was very limited navigational equipment. Weather also played a major part in accidents. Forecasts were far less accurate than they are today, and it was not unusual for aircraft to arrive at a given destination and find that the TAF (Terminal Aerodrome Forecast) was completely different from what the crews now faced. The pilots then faced a dilemma over whether to try to land or divert to another destination, which may be some distance away, with perhaps limited fuel reserves. Many other major carriers faced similar operating conditions and suffered losses, so Varig was by no means unique in this respect.

The Coronavirus pandemic has probably had the greatest effect on the airline industry since its inception, and had Varig survived after 2006, it is doubtful whether it would still be in business today. Of Varig's rivals, only TAM continues to exist, although it is now in a completely different form and known as LATAM (since 2016), and significant parts of its routes are in Chile and Paraguay. VASP went out of business on 27 January 2005, and, for a number of years, its fleet of 27 aircraft was stored at Congonhas airport in São Paulo, before most were broken up. Of TransBrasil, there is no trace. The airline declared bankruptcy following the grounding of its fleet on 3 December 2001. It was finally declared bankrupt in 2003 at the request of one of its major debtors, the US leasing company GE Capital Aviation Services. However, the bankruptcy was not confirmed by the Brazilian Federal Supreme Court until 2 October 2009.

Many of the major international carriers survive, but the first class and, to some extent, the business class cabins are largely empty. The sale and use of business jets has risen exponentially during and since the pandemic, and some carriers are seriously considering reducing the premium space on their aircraft. The airline business has changed beyond recognition, and many of the airlines which offered such high standards of service, the so-called 'Legacy Carriers', are no longer with us; it may well be that Varig's story will not be the last like this to be told.

Author's Note

It is clear that the final months of Varig became very complicated, with claim and counterclaim, and judicial proceedings overturning or altering previous decisions. A number of organisations entered the marketplace to buy what remained of the airline. Some were successful, others were not. The end result was that Varig ceased to exist as an airline.

Using the internet and local sources, both in English and Portuguese, I have tried to piece together the story as I understand it. I realise that this may not reflect all the activities that took place at the time, or that there may be inaccuracies in the way they have been written. It is very difficult to find a definition of precisely what did happen during and after the splitting up of the airline, but I have made my best efforts to explain the process. Any inaccuracies in the narrative are a result of my inability to examine all the factors which came about in the demise of the airline.

Other books you might like:

Historic Commercial Aircraft
Series, Vol. 3

Airlines Series, Vol. 4

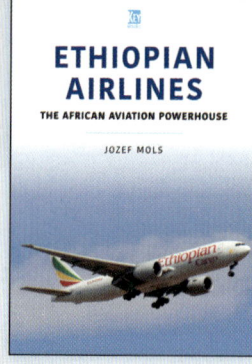

Airlines Series, Vol. 2

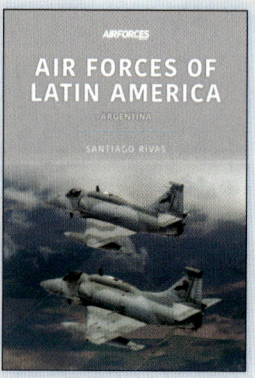

Air Forces Series, Vol. 1

Airlines Series, Vol. 1

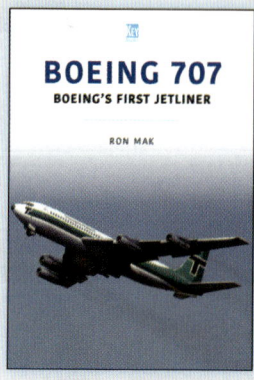

Historic Commercial
Aircraft Series, Vol. 2

For our full range of titles please visit:
shop.keypublishing.com/books

VIP Book Club

Sign up today and receive
TWO FREE E-BOOKS

Be the first to find out about our forthcoming
book releases and receive exclusive offers.

Register now at keypublishing.com/vip-book-club

Our VIP Book Club is a 100% spam-free zone, and we will never share your email with anyone else.
You can read our full privacy policy at: privacy.keypublishing.com